MOBILE STRATEGIES
for DIGITAL PUBLISHING

MOBILE STRATEGIES

A Practical Guide to the Evolving Landscape

Thad McIlroy

THE FUTURE OF PUBLISHING

Copyright © 2015 by Thad McIlroy & Digital Book World. All rights reserved. Published by The Future of Publishing and Digital Book World, an imprint of F+W Media, Inc., 10151 Carver Road, Suite #200, Blue Ash, OH 45242. Second edition, with minor revisions, published February, 2015.

ISBN: 978-1-4403-4326-1 (PDF)
ISBN: 978-1-4403-4325-4 (EPUB & Kindle Mobi)
ISBN: 978-0-9813608-2-9 (Paperback)

No part of this publication may be reproduced or transmitted in any form or by any means, electronic or mechanical, including photocopy, or any information storage and retrieval system, without written permission of the copyright holders. Contact Thad McIlroy at thad@thefutureofpublishing.com.

Author: Thad McIlroy
Editors: Rich Bellis, Jeremy Greenfield,
Cover Design: Danielle Fluegeman
Book Design: Kelsey Erck
Project Sponsorship: Integra Software Services Pvt. Ltd.

TABLE OF CONTENTS

Introduction 1

1. The Mobile Opportunity Told in Key Stats...........................9
2. Mobile Strategies for Content..53
3. Tools for Building Ebooks and Apps 63
4. Mobile Marketing Strategies 75
5. Case Studies: Publishing Goes Mobile.............................101
6. The Future of Mobile for Digital Publishers 115
   Glossary 119
   Additional Resources 125
   About the Author.. 129
   About the Sponsor... 130

INTRODUCTION

For publishers, mobile is a foreign country. The inhabitants are shiny new devices, smartphones, tablets and e-readers—not to mention apps, the strange new beasts that live among them. Mobile is exploding faster than any communications technology that preceded it. Everywhere you look people are glued to their devices. Chances are they won't come unglued anytime soon.

And yet in many ways, "mobile" is a fiction. As publishers, authors, technologists and content creators, we make a mistake if we treat mobile as something wholly distinct from desktop computers. And we make another mistake when we treat it as separate from TV, gaming and music or video streaming. Mobile is intertwined with everything we do in digital entertainment—whether shopping, computing, communicating or just being social.

Mobile Strategies for Digital Publishing looks at each of the switches that can move the mobile dial within the digital publishing ecosystem. But just as often, this report will show when moving mobile switches also moves other mechanisms. After all, mobile is not a species. It's an ecosphere.

The challenges mobile presents can be tough to grasp because definitions are still evolving. A [report from Monetate](#) notes:

> Consumers most often associate "mobile" with a smartphone/cell phone (54% selected this association), while only 14% said tablets/e-readers. 32% also said they associate mobile with ease of use on the go, demonstrating that consumers feel a strong link between that device in their pockets and the connected freedom it brings.

In the modern era, book publishing has always competed for attention with other print and audio/visual media: newspapers and magazines; recorded music; radio; television; and feature films. But never has book publishing competed with these media on the exact same devices. The battle for attention, eyeballs and dollars has never been so intense.

The publishing industry is now adept at delivering content to mobile devices as ebooks. But mobile is not mainly about reading. For users, smartphones are primarily about texting and social networking and online gaming. Tablet users connect over similar software, while ultra-high-resolution screens make tablets perfect for watching movies and videos. Both smartphones and tablets feature digital cameras that can shoot still images and record video. [One analyst estimates](#) that total photo sharing across all social networks will be over 1 trillion images in 2014.

It's within this media mix that ebooks are ever more intimately situated. As a result, ebooks offer book publishers a modest but profitable toe in the water toward a mobile publishing future, at a time when sales of ebook may be approaching the limits of their growth. And while it's uncertain just how much enhanced ebooks and apps will fuel the next phase in content sales, writing and reading still enjoy unprecedented popularity as mobile growth accelerates. The audience is out there. The challenge for book publishers is to align their content and business models with mobile's vast opportunities.

HOW WE GOT HERE

The best way to visualize the opportunity in mobile is to return to the days before the World Wide Web. In the early '90s getting online meant dialing directly into the network of a service like America Online (AOL). Network speeds were slow but easy access to email was the big draw. Over time, AOL added content "channels" to its network—content that AOL selected for its customers.

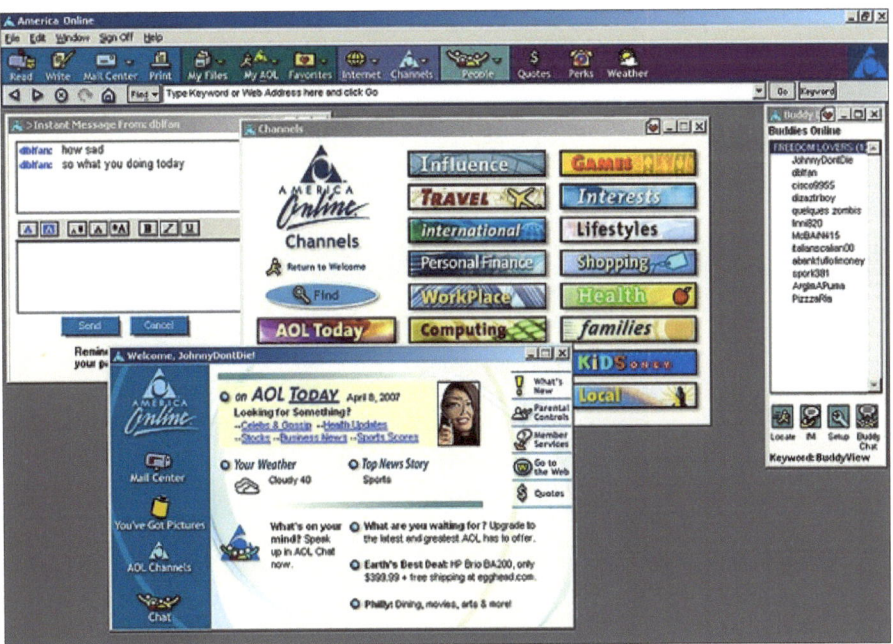

Source: Mashable

In late 1994, Netscape introduced the first web browser, effectively breaking AOL's closed-network model. Users now accessed the web without a gatekeeper. By the early 2000s fast broadband service at home turned web browsing into entertainment.

Mobile, meanwhile, began as "cell phones" without web access. Sometime after the year 2000 Personal Digital Assistants (PDAs), most running Microsoft software, represented a big leap forward. Their operating systems controlled the user interface in ways similar to AOL's early hold on PCs.

Source: Softonic

The 2007 introduction of Apple's iPhone ushered in the era of the smartphone. Touch screens replaced cursors and keyboards. Apps replaced the network interface. Built-in cameras snapped photos and recorded video that soon rivaled standalone digital cameras. Wifi provided low-cost network access. Social networking was ideally suited to these carry-along devices. And smartphones soon became location-aware, ushering in a new category of apps.

Smartphones today have the same computing power as the PCs of 2005. Multiple sensors are transforming smartphones into intelligent devices. By 2012, phone calls accounted for less than 10% smartphone use.

TABLETS AND MOBILE

Tablets float in the tightening space between smartphones and PCs. They're squeezed from both sides. On one side are smartphones with oversized screens, so-called "phablets." On the other side are notebook PCs, [Chromebooks](#) and [tablet/keyboard combos](#). Despite their huge installed base, tablets sometimes look like transitional devices.

The high contrast and low glare of black-and-white e-readers still make them the first choice for the most devoted bibliophiles. The attraction of tablets as e-readers stems mostly from their additional functionality, which is ideal for games and video.

Web browsing works on tablets but feels crowded on smartphones, unless the site publisher offers a special smartphone-optimized version.

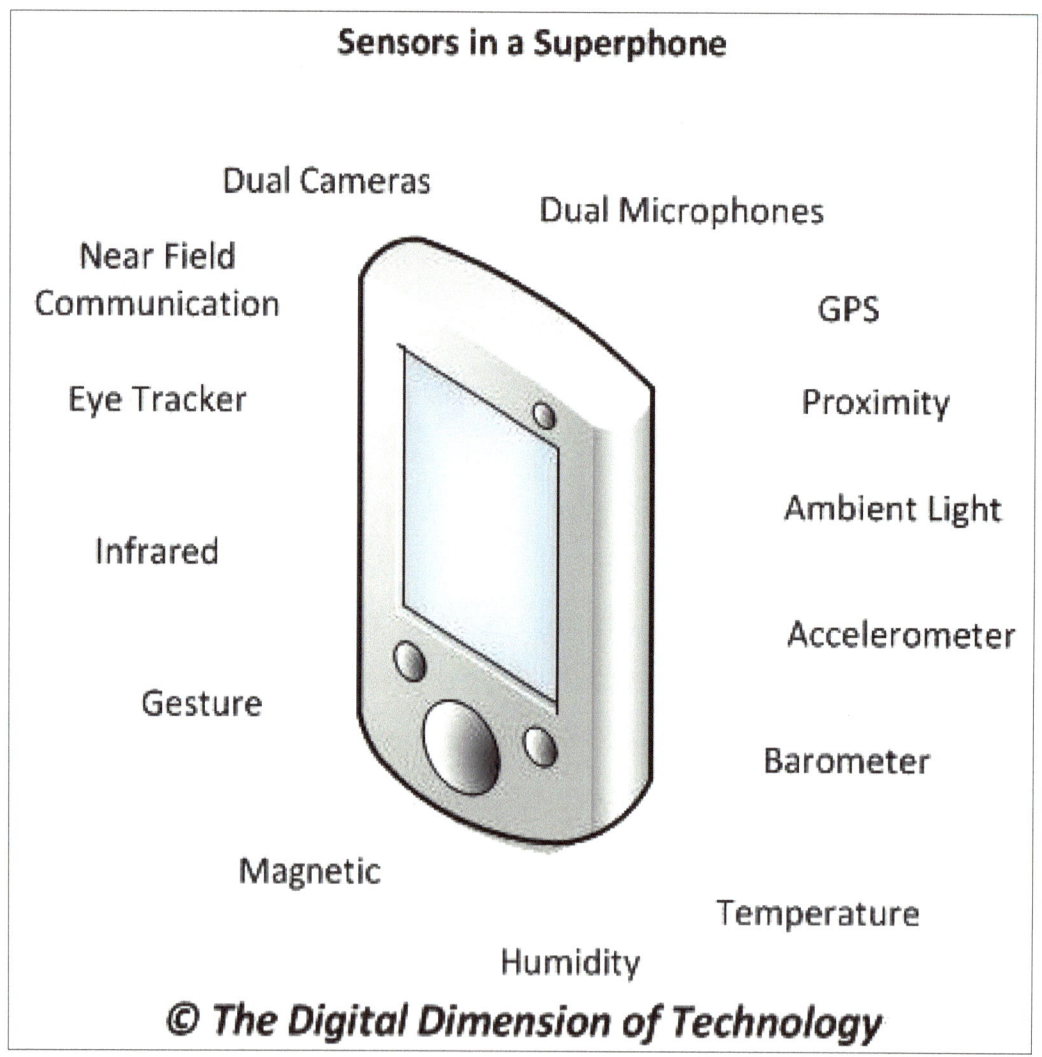

Source: The Digital Dimension of Technology

HOW TO USE THIS REPORT

Mobile Strategies for Digital Publishing provides a snapshot of the fast-developing mobile landscape and the range of mobile strategies for book publishers. While this report's title emphasizes digital publishing, the opportunities it explores also include the marketing and sale of print books via mobile devices.

First, a few definitions and clarifications. *Mobile Strategies for Digital Publishing* classifies both smartphones and tablets as mobile devices. When discussing just one or the other, the term "smartphone" or "tablet" marks the distinction. "Cell phones" (also known as "feature phones") crop up occasionally, indicating the generation of devices before smartphones, lacking touch screens and the wide range of smartphone apps.

Ebook readers (e-readers) are also mobile media devices. They're portable and connect to wireless networks. E-reader use has leveled off as those devices are supplanted by more versatile tablets. Still, they remain the No. 1 mobile device for ebook reading and buying. They are featured in the report wherever there's data available and something noteworthy to say.

The extent of the explosion in mobile technology has been thoroughly documented. Chapter 1 assembles the latest data on the depth and breadth of mobile's growth, tying those statistics into current publishing industry trends in, and approaches to, mobile content and marketing.

Chapters 2 and 3 focus on how content choices affect mobile strategies. Chapter 4 drills down to the tactical level of mobile marketing.

Chapter 5 features case studies and examples of enhanced ebooks and apps.

Mobile Strategies for Digital Publishing wraps up with a glimpse of what the future holds at the intersection of mobile and digital publishing (Chapter 6).

Supplemental materials include a glossary and a list of additional resources.

The report was written primarily for online publication. There are valuable hyperlinks throughout linking sources used by author in the research and writing of the report.

If you have purchased the print version of the report and would like to receive a copy of a digital version contact me at thad@thefutureofpublishing.com. Please tell me *where you purchased the print book from* and then specify which file format you would like to receive, along with your email. I will send it to you without charge, and will protect the privacy of your email address.

CHAPTER 1
THE MOBILE OPPORTUNITY TOLD IN KEY STATS

The best way to understand the mobile opportunity is to absorb some of the data that defines today's mobile market. Gathered here are more than thirty charts offering a broad range of statistics and trends. Together they reveal how essential mobile is to publishing. There's a breathless quality to many of the mobile industry's reports, but taken together, a profile of the broader market opportunity takes shape.

Most mobile data ignores dedicated e-readers. The section below, "Quantifying E-Reading Devices," fills in the details.

If you prefer to cut to the chase, the last section of this chapter, "What Do the Charts Tell Us?" summarizes the most important and the least expected lessons.

THE STUNNING GROWTH OF MOBILE

Cell phone adoption grew faster than did all the computer, communications and entertainment technologies that preceded it. An often-updated chart illustrates the relative adoption curves.

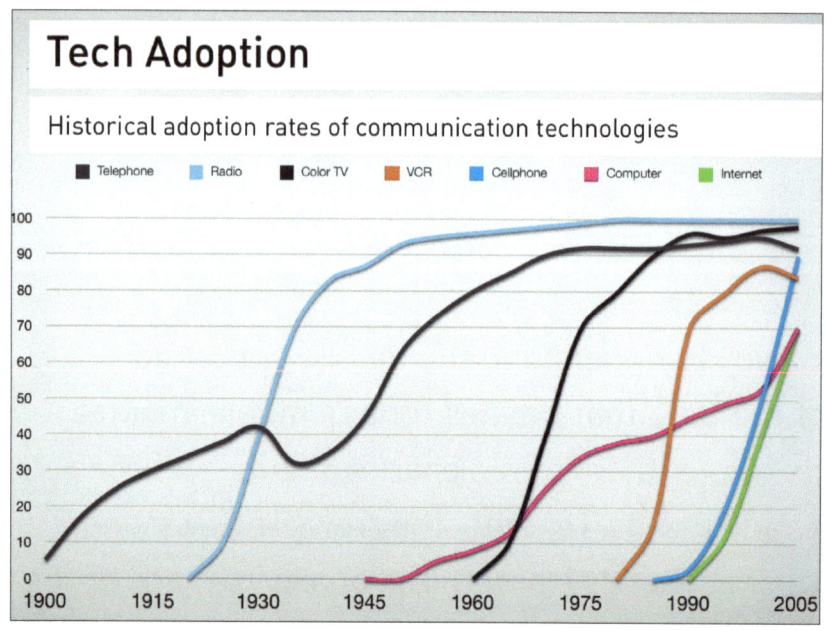

Source: Peter Leyden

Analyst Benedict Evans developed this chart comparing unit sales of PCs to sales of smartphones and tablets. It shows that annual mobile unit sales overtook PC sales after 2011.

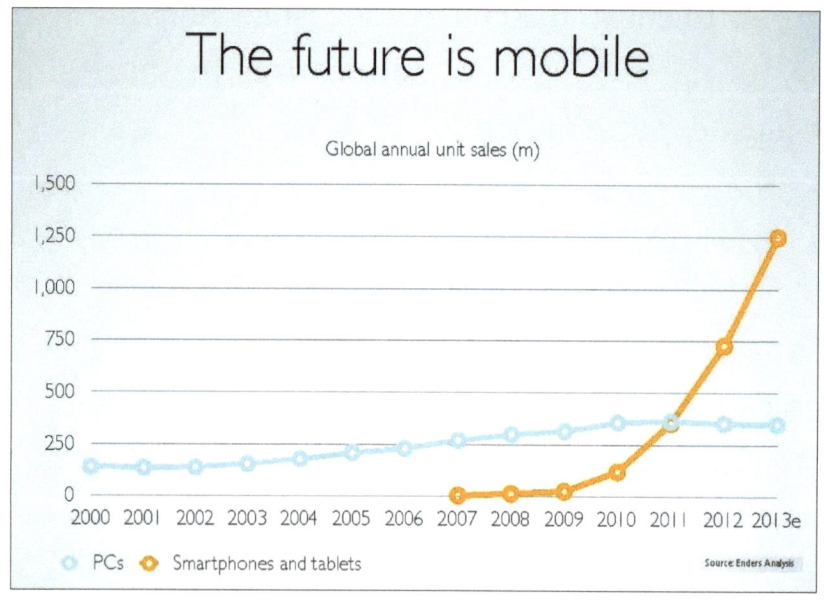

Source: Enders Analysis

Evans predicted in December 2013 that during the following six months "the number of smartphones on Earth will pass the number of PCs."

Asymco data indicates that there are now some 175 million smartphone users in the U.S. and that by the end of 2020 nearly 100% of people older than 13 will be using a smartphone.

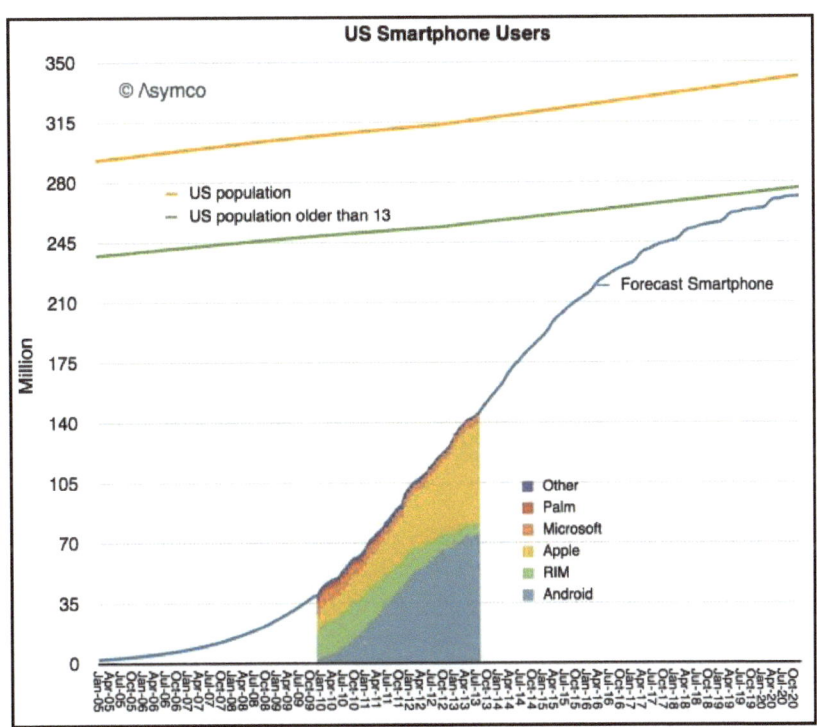

Source: Asymco

Tablet adoption has grown even faster than smartphones, although tablets are unlikely to reach the same market saturation; phones remain smaller, cheaper and more useful for a broader range of applications than tablets. ABI estimates that the installed base for tablets in the U.S. was 70 million units at the end of 2013.

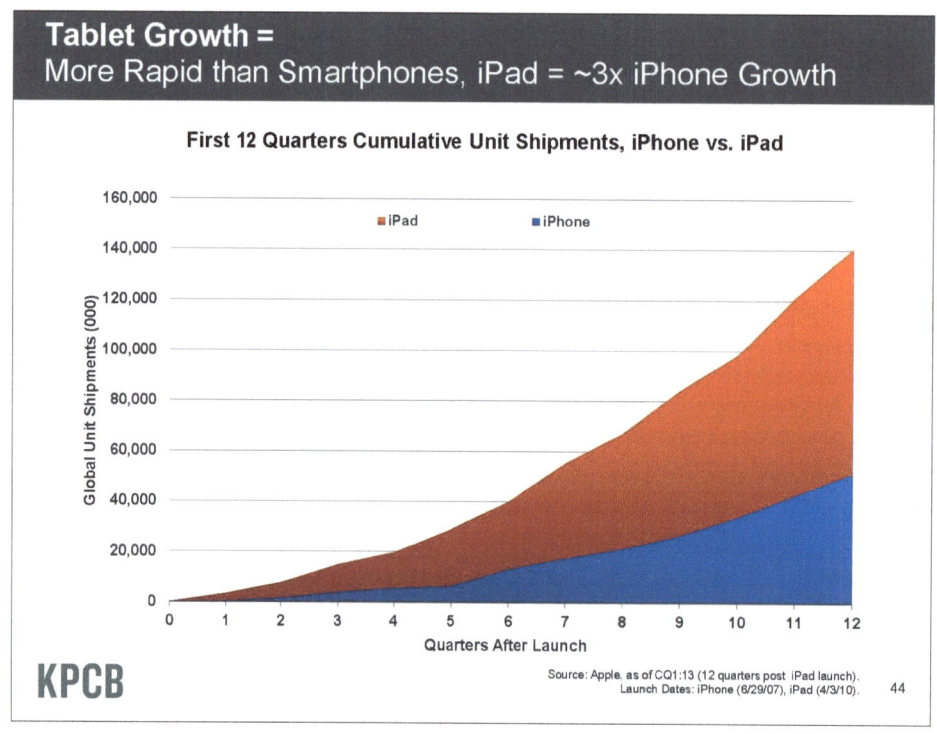

Source: Mary Meeker, KPCB

Smartphones have nearly twice the U.S. installed base as do tablets.

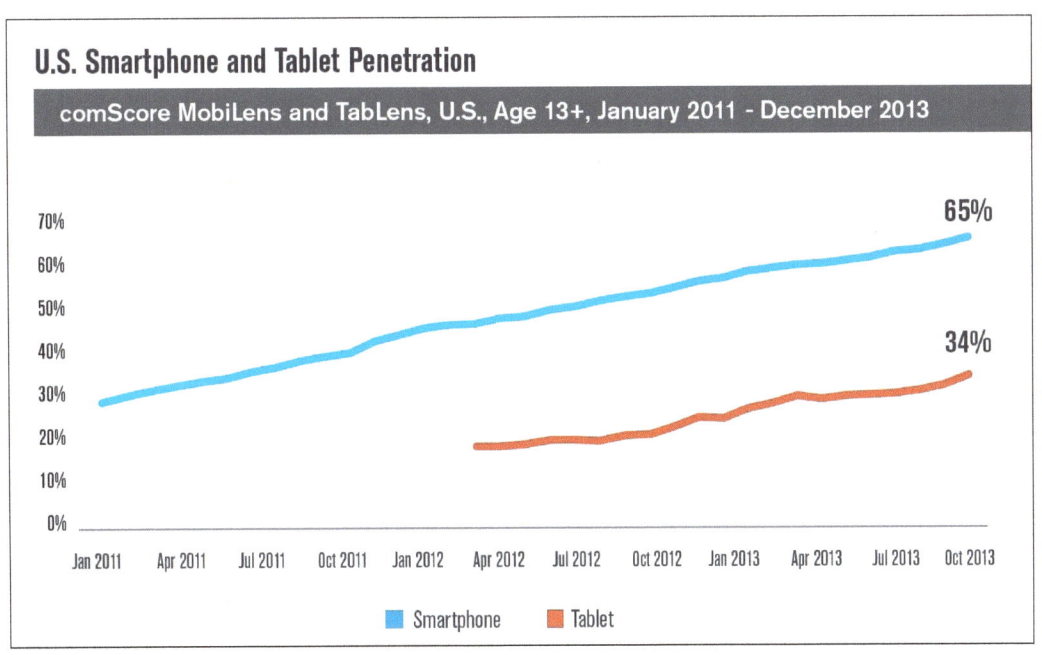

Source: comScore

Meanwhile, the loud explosion in tablet sales is growing quiet. Sales in "mature markets" were forecast to grow by just 3.1% in 2014.

Tom Mainelli at IDC notes that "two major issues are causing the tablet market to slow down. First, consumers are keeping their tablets, especially higher-cost models from major vendors, far longer than originally anticipated… Second, the rise of phablets—smartphones with 5.5-inch and larger screens—are causing many people to second-guess tablet purchases, as the larger screens on these phones are often adequate for tasks once reserved for tablets."

At issue for publishers is that it's only *the growth* in sales that's slowing. Apple will still ship some 55 million new iPads this year, and many of those will be heading to new customers, rather than serving as upgrades for existing iPad fans. And so the iPad tablet opportunity remains large and still growing.

The explosion in mobile is having an impact on PC sales. IDC data confirms that PC sales growth dropped into negative territory in 2012. Still, 300 million PCs shipped in 2013 to an installed based estimated at somewhere between 800 million and 1.1 billion. And separately "Gartner reported that worldwide PC shipments increased 0.1% in the second quarter, the first after two years of declining shipments."

It's tempting to imagine that mobile devices might replace PCs altogether, but a 2013 IDC survey found that "only 8.7% of tablet buyers want to use the tablet as a replacement for their laptops."

TAKEAWAYS FOR PUBLISHERS

Mobile adoption is exploding on both smartphones and tablets while PC sales growth slows. The charts below offer a more detailed look at the mobile opportunity.

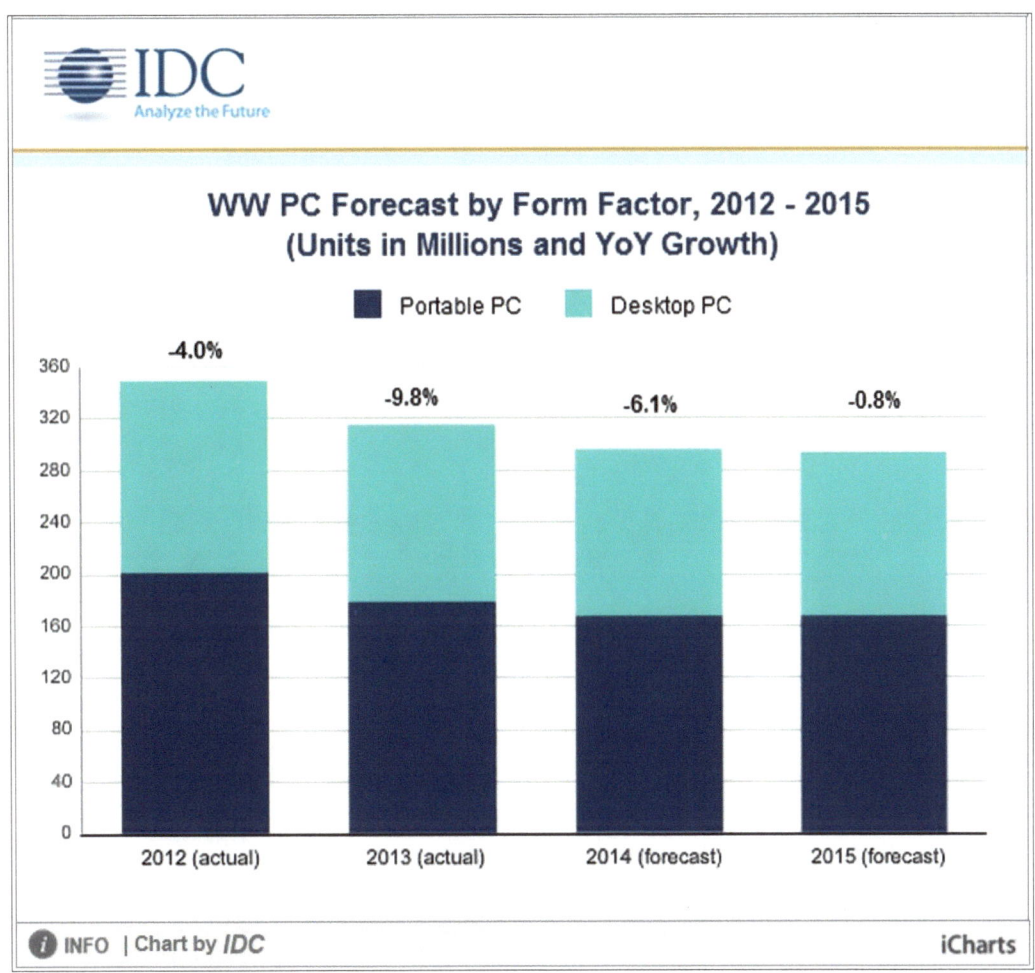

Source: IDC

APPLE VERSUS ANDROID

SMARTPHONES

Mobile is not a single market. It is partly divided by the device—smartphones, tablets and e-readers. It's divided again by the operating system of the major devices—Apple iOS or Google's

Android. (E-readers have much simpler proprietary operating software that's not relevant to this discussion).

Many reports show that Android increasingly ranks as the top smartphone platform worldwide.

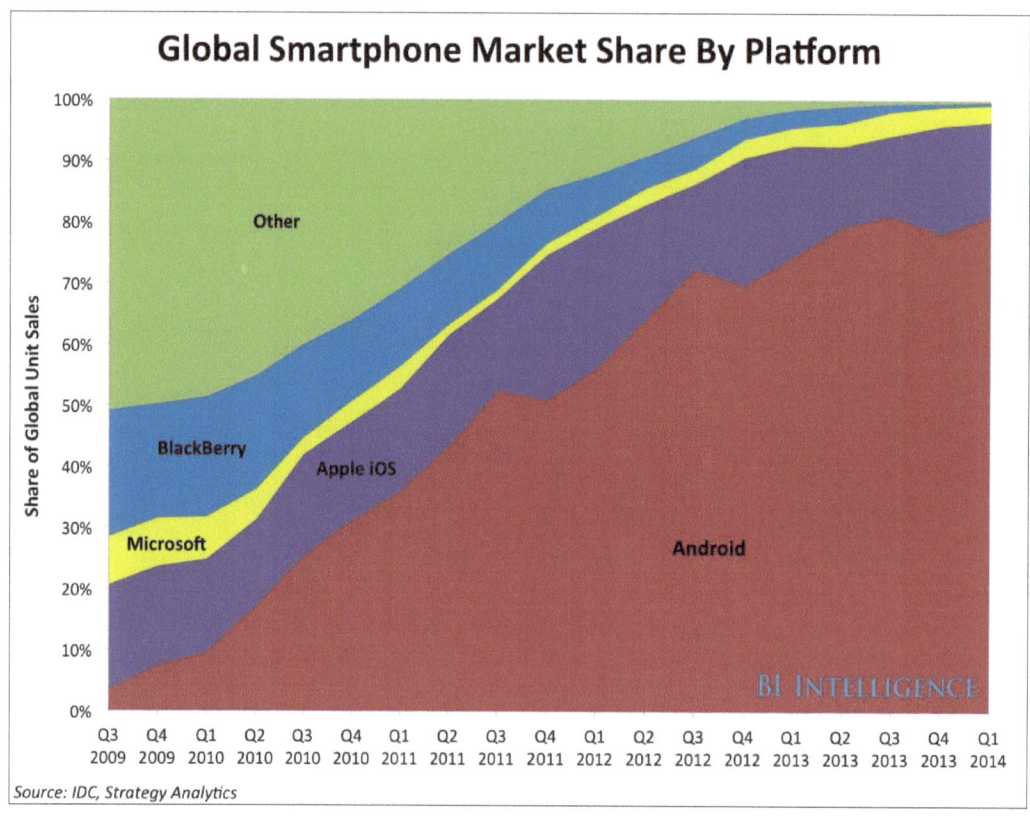

Source: BI Intelligence

Android is also No. 1 in the U.S. but by a slimmer margin. (And Apple's continues to play cat and mouse: February 2015 stats show Apple once again ahead.)

Top Smartphone Platforms 3 Month Avg. Ending Aug. 2014 vs. 3 Month Avg. Ending May 2014 Total U.S. Smartphone Subscribers Age 13+ Source: comScore MobiLens			
	Share (%) of Smartphone Subscribers		
	May-14	Aug-14	Point Change
Total Smartphone Subscribers	100.0%	100.0%	N/A
Android	52.1%	52.0%	-0.1
Apple	41.9%	42.0%	0.1
Microsoft	3.4%	3.5%	0.1
BlackBerry	2.3%	2.3%	0.0
Symbian	0.1%	0.1%	0.0

Source: comScore

TABLETS

In tablets the story is different. There's the Apple iPad, and then there's everyone else. The iPad has nearly 60% of the installed base of U.S. tablet users. ([ABI Research assigns](#) to Apple 51% of worldwide tablet market share as of December 2013.)

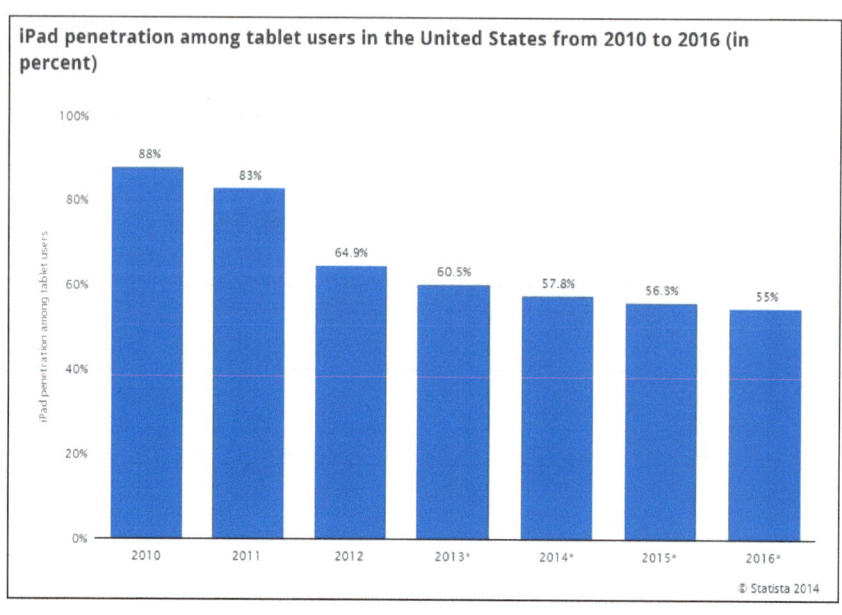

Source: Statista

iPad users are more engaged by their devices than other tablet users; in this respect, too, iPads dwarf the other players. Measured by the volume of web traffic driven by tablets, iPads accounted for over three-quarters of tablet use (U.S. and Canada).

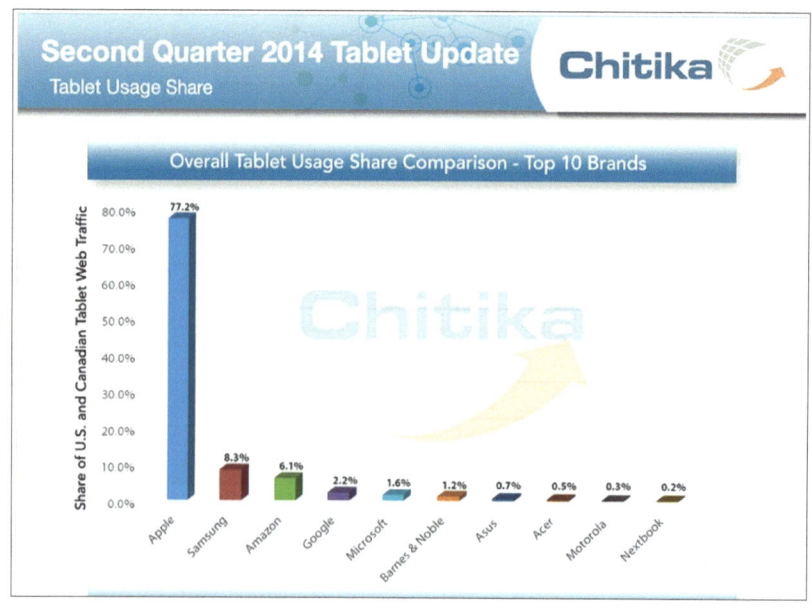

Source: Chitika

Analyst Ben Evans posits that it "may be better to think of tablets, laptops and desktops as one 'big screen' segment, all of which compete with smartphones, and for which the opportunity is just smaller than that for smartphones." Over time tablets will eat at laptop PC sales just as laptops ate at desktop PC sales. But, he states, "The truly transformative new category is the smartphone."

USAGE PATTERNS

The behavior of Apple mobile users differs from Android users. One consequence is that Apple devices command higher revenue per user than do Android.

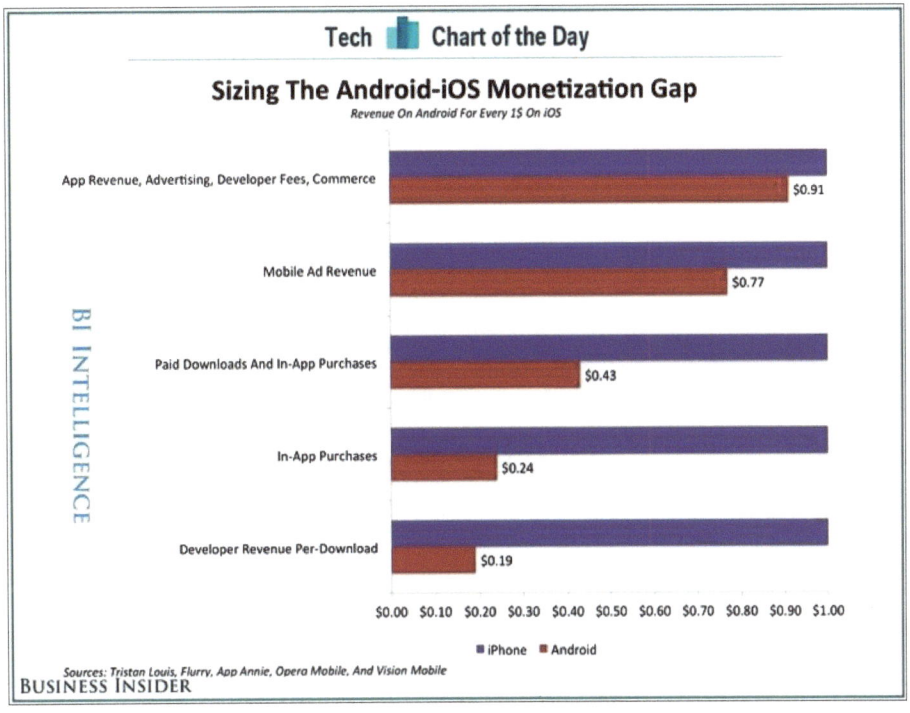

Source: BI Intelligence

For instance, iPhone users are willing to pay a higher retail price for apps.

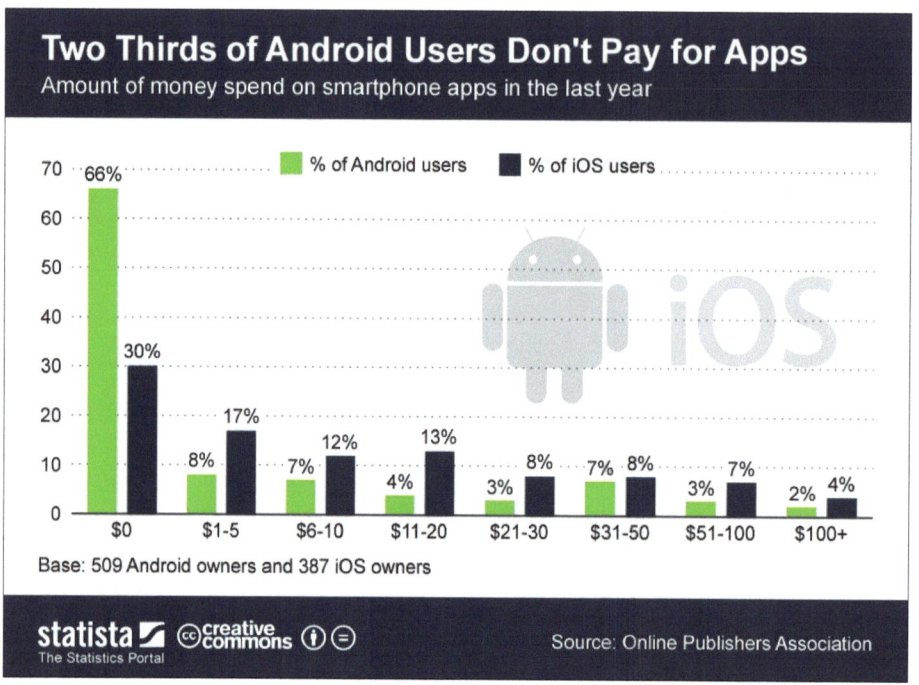

Source: Online Publishers Association, Statista

Cyber Monday, the year's top day for online shopping, accentuated the revenue gap in favor of Apple mobile users: last fall they spent five-and-a-half times more than Android mobile users.

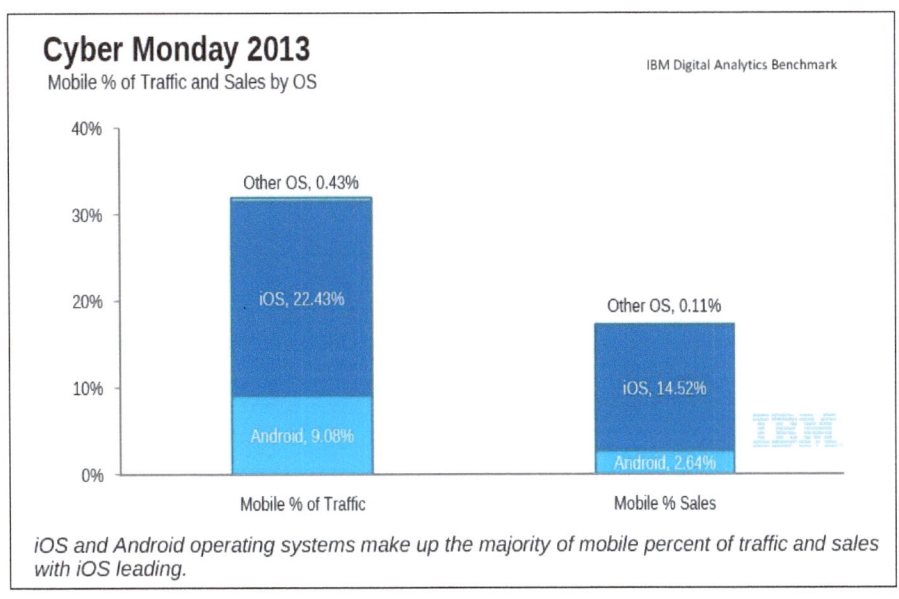

Source: IBM Digital Analytics

The revenue gap extended to money spent at retailers via smartphones and tablets. Smartphones generated more traffic, but tablets drove more than double the percentage of sales.

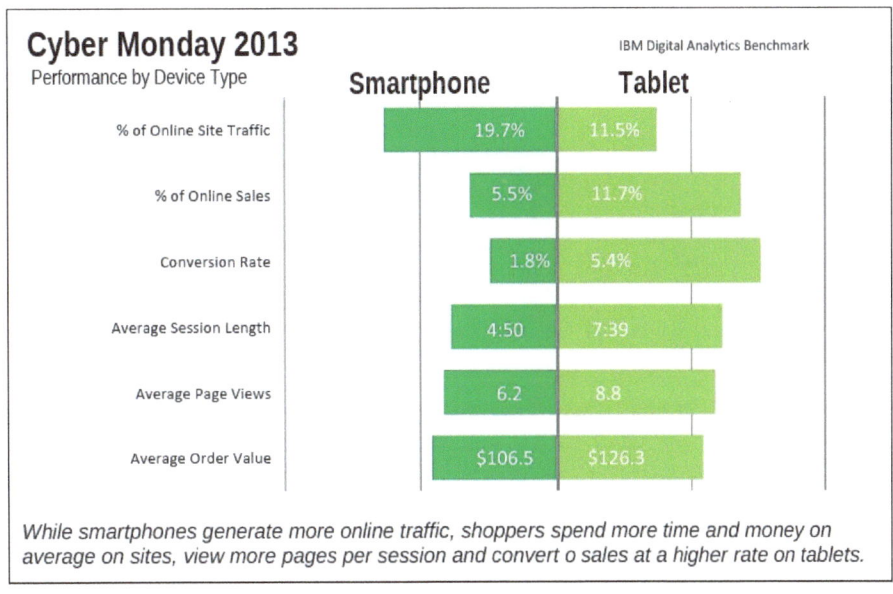

Source: IBM Digital Analytics

When measured more broadly, tablets have fallen behind smartphones for retail spending. Regardless, PCs still dominate e-commerce by a large margin.

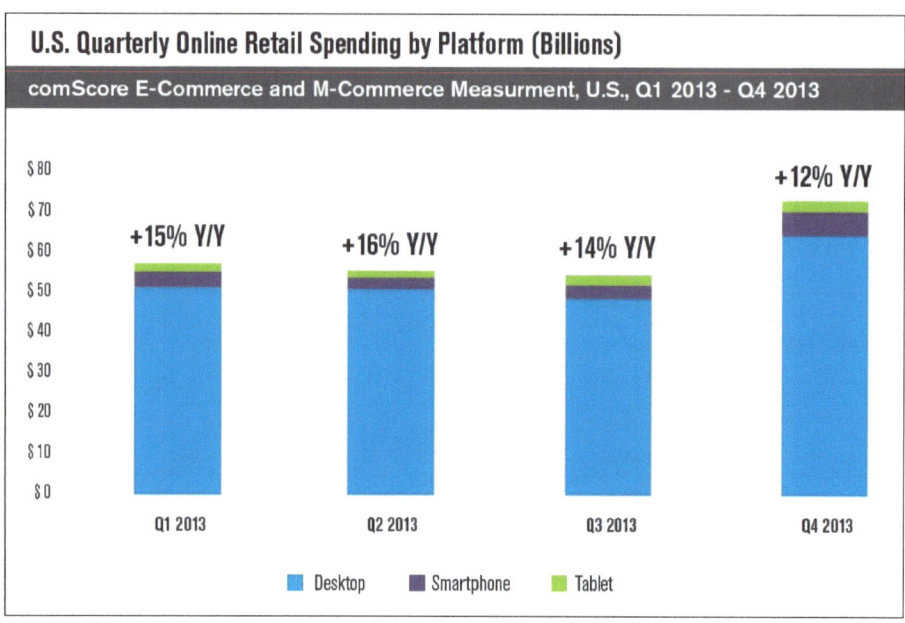

Source: comScore

Smartphones are far more plentiful than tablets, but a Monetate report shows that tablets drive 40% more web traffic than smartphones (while PCs still command nearly three-quarters of website visits).

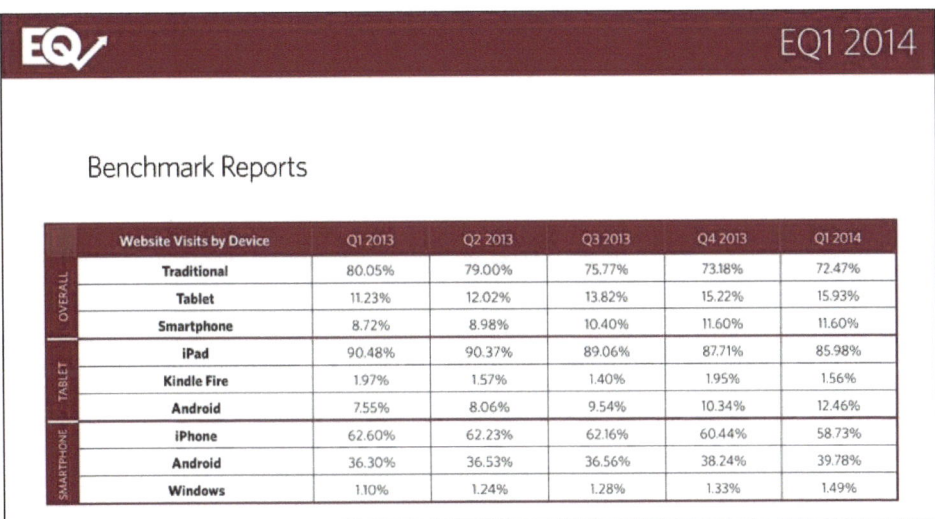

Source: Monetate Ecommerce Quarterly

TAKEAWAYS FOR PUBLISHERS

The charts above provide a glimpse into one of the most vexing challenges for app developers: Which are more important, Apple devices or Android ones? Android now wins the "total installed base" of smartphones contest while Apple continues to dominate the U.S. tablet market.

Apple iOS users spend more on just about everything, from mobile apps to the online commerce mediated by those apps. But it's foolhardy to focus exclusively on Apple mobile. The gap is closing, and mainstream app developers now take Android as seriously as iOS.

While tablets and smartphones are often lumped together into "mobile," smartphone use is different from tablet use. The larger tablet displays make them better suited to visiting websites than do the small screen real estate on smartphones. Tablets are also the mobile platform driving big-ticket online sales but no longer comprise the bulk of mobile online sales volume. PCs continue to dwarf mobile online spend, commanding as much as 90% of the total.

MOBILE APPS AND HOW THEY'RE USED

Life would be so much easier for publishers if mobile users still "surfed the web" rather than launching apps. But apps maintain their mastery on mobile. In fact, apps gained six points in the percentage of mobile time spent over the last year. This puts to rest any question of whether publishers can create a sufficient mobile reach *solely* through their websites.

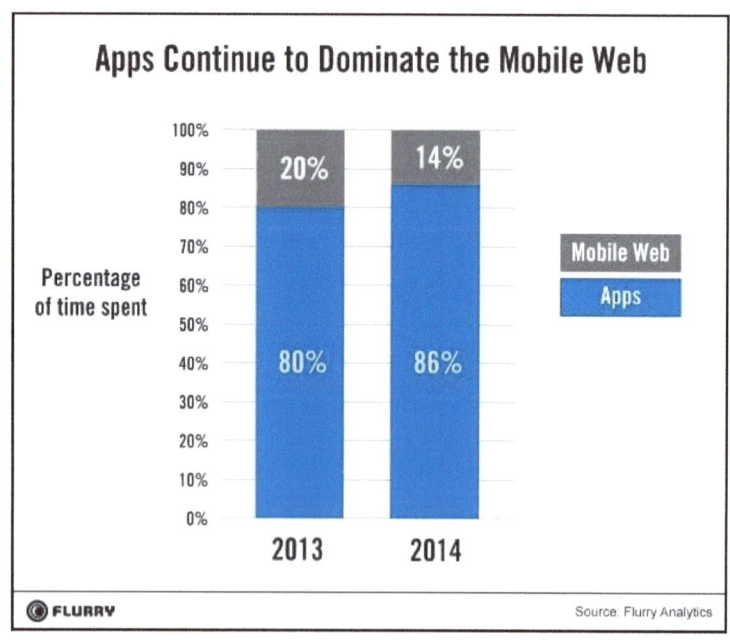

Source: Flurry Analytics

It's worth bearing in mind that the average adult spent two hours and twenty-one minutes per day on mobile devices (phones and tablets) in 2013. Mobile web use accounts for about a half-hour per day. That data is consistent with a separate study by the Donald W. Reynolds Journalism Institute (data for web use on tablets was essentially the same).

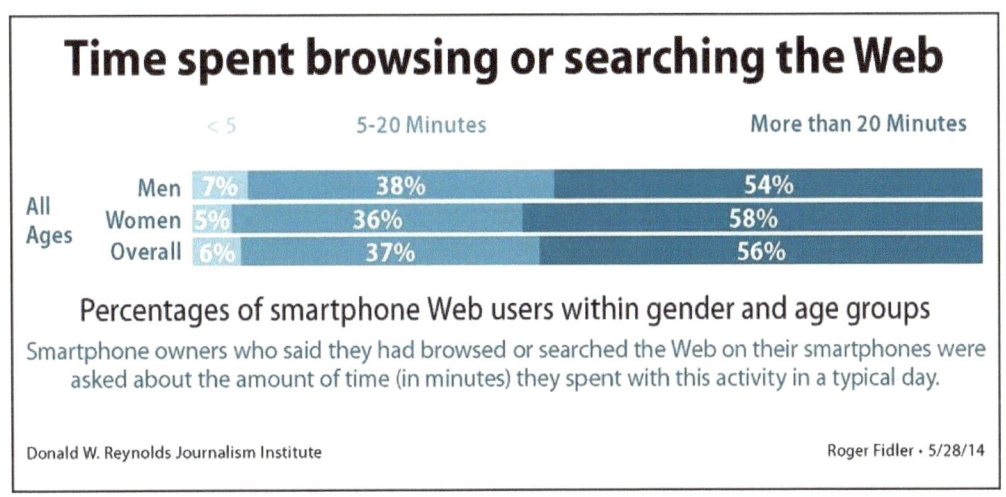

Source: Donald W. Reynolds Journalism Institute

Stuck behind gaming and social apps, entertainment (including publishing) plays a small role in the mobile universe.

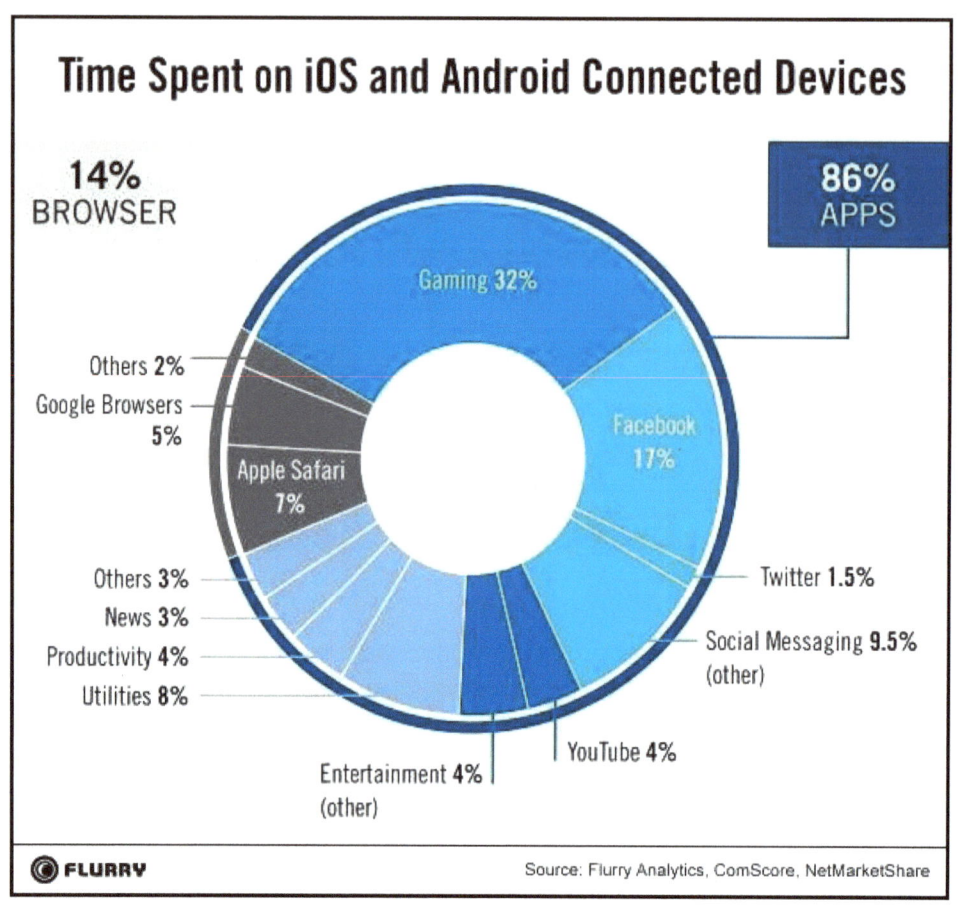

Source: Flurry Analytics, comScore, NetMarketShare

These charts from Nielsen's February 2014 Digital Consumer Report illustrate how compelling social is for smartphone users. They also show that social media attention is garnered via apps—the second chart notes how little time is spent accessing social media via web browsers.

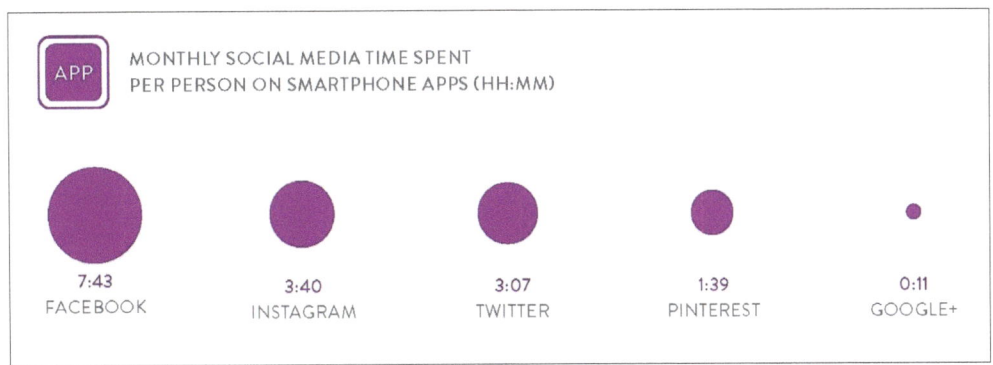

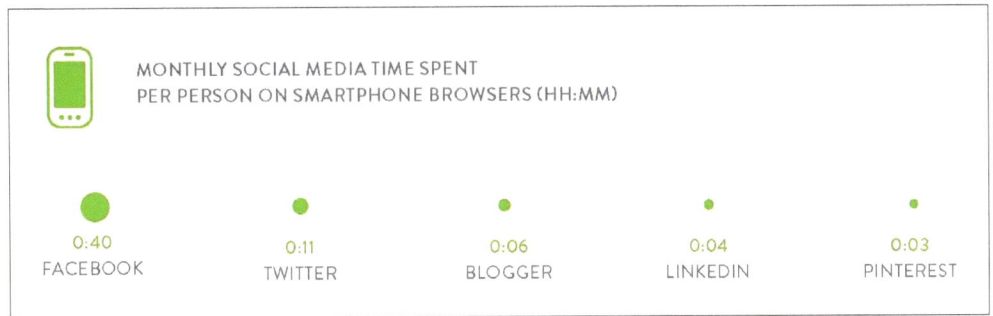

Source: Nielsen

As TechCrunch reported, "at Apple's Worldwide Developer's Conference the company announced that the iOS App Store has now reached 1.2 million apps—a staggering number that puts Apple neck-and-neck with competitor Google, which is currently estimated to have roughly 1.2 million."

The chart below puts these numbers into perspective: The fifteen apps listed are used by between a fifth and three-quarters of all mobile users. The other 1,199,985 apps compete for users' reduced attention.

Top 15 Smartphone Apps April 2014 Total U.S. Smartphone Mobile Media Users, Age 18+ (iOS and Android Platforms) Source: comScore Mobile Metrix		
	Top 15 Apps	% Reach
	Smartphone App Audience	100.0%
1	Facebook (Mobile App)	74.1%
2	Google Play (Mobile App)	50.9%
3	YouTube (Mobile App)	49.7%
4	Google Search (Mobile App)	48.3%
5	Pandora Radio (Mobile App)	44.9%
6	Gmail (Mobile App)	41.6%
7	Google Maps (Mobile App)	41.5%
8	Yahoo Stocks (Mobile App)	30.0%
9	Instagram (Mobile App)	29.3%
10	Facebook Messenger (Mobile App)	26.7%
11	Yahoo Weather Widget (Mobile App)	26.6%
12	Apple Maps (Mobile App)	24.5%
13	iTunes Radio/iCloud (Mobile App)	21.5%
14	Twitter (Mobile App)	20.4%
15	The Weather Channel (Mobile App)	20.1%

Source: comScore

Another chart illustrates how rapidly Facebook users have shifted to mobile.

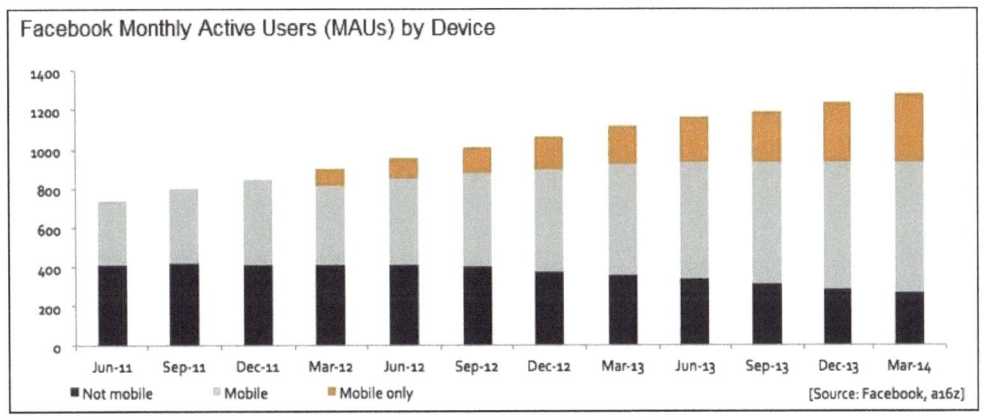

Source: Benedict Evans

In its first quarter financial report in 2014 Facebook anticipated that "mobile usage will continue to be the primary driver of our user growth for the foreseeable future and that usage through personal computers *will decline worldwide*, including in key markets such as the United States and other developed markets in Europe and Asia" (emphasis mine).

It's not just Facebook that's moving to mobile. The chart below compares mobile-to-desktop use for all the major social networks. Only LinkedIn and Tumblr maintain more desktop than mobile users.

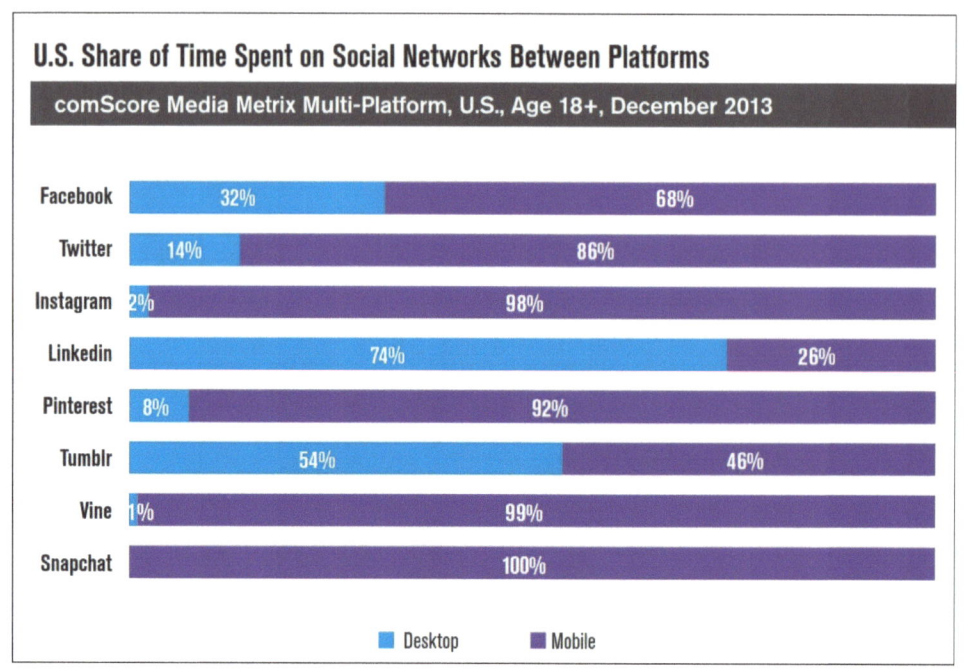

Source: comScore

TAKEAWAYS FOR PUBLISHERS

Apps dominate the world of mobile and do so increasingly. Website visits account for only 14% of mobile time spent. A book publisher's mobile strategy must include an app strategy. That doesn't mean publishers must create apps. Interacting with mobile means reaching users through the most popular apps already in use, including Facebook, Twitter, Instagram and perhaps a dozen others.

OUR LIVES ONSCREEN

Google's data indicates that people are spending an astonishing four-and-a-half hours of their daily leisure time in front of a screen. Only 10% of media encounters are non-screen-based, including both print and radio.

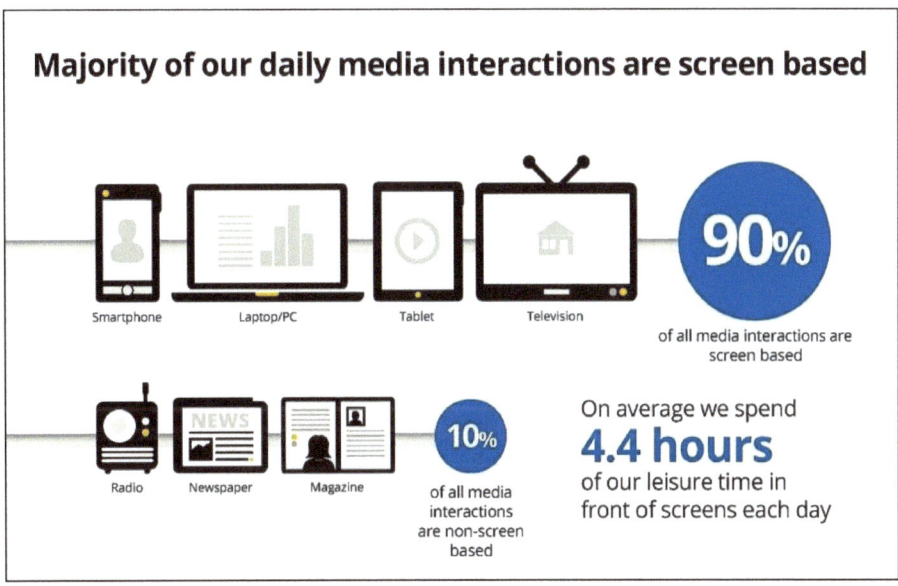

Source: Google

ComScore uncovered a surprising phenomenon: time spent on mobile doesn't appear to be taking away from PC use, and certainly not from TV watching. The time spent with mobile devices is incremental to other screen interactions.

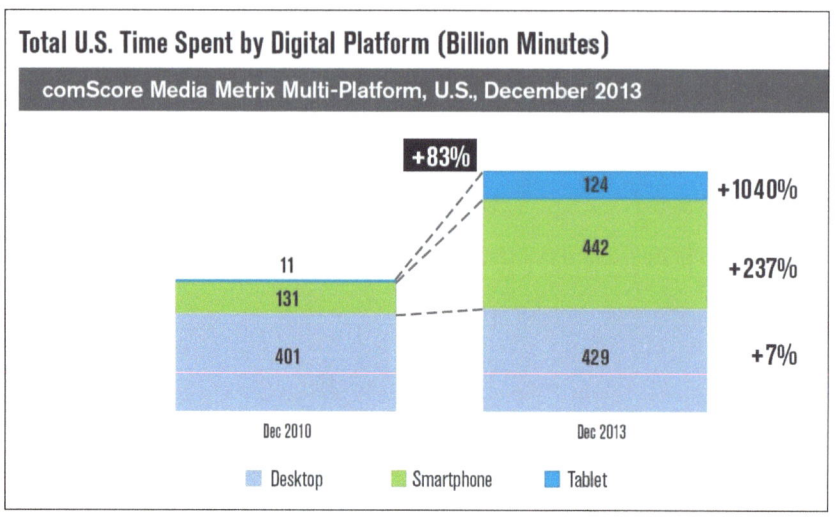

Source: comScore

The U.S. Department of Labor's American Time Use Study paints another picture of media interaction in relation to other leisure activities. "Reading" accounts for a mere 20 minutes (7%) of the 5.1 daily hours devoted to leisure and sports .

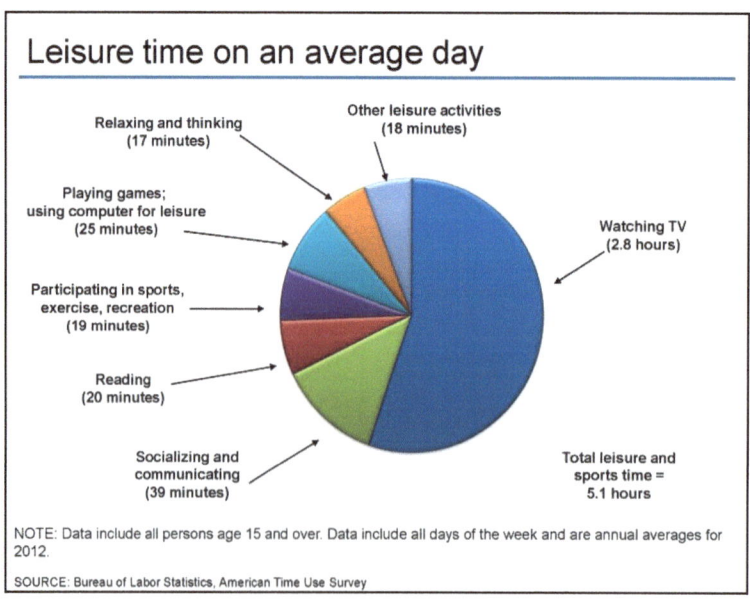

Source: U.S. Bureau of Labor Statistics

The survey notes that "individuals age 75 and over averaged 1 hour of reading per weekend day…while individuals ages 15 to 19 read for an average of 7 minutes per weekend day."

It remains to be seen whether 15–19 year-olds will morph into heavier readers as they age.

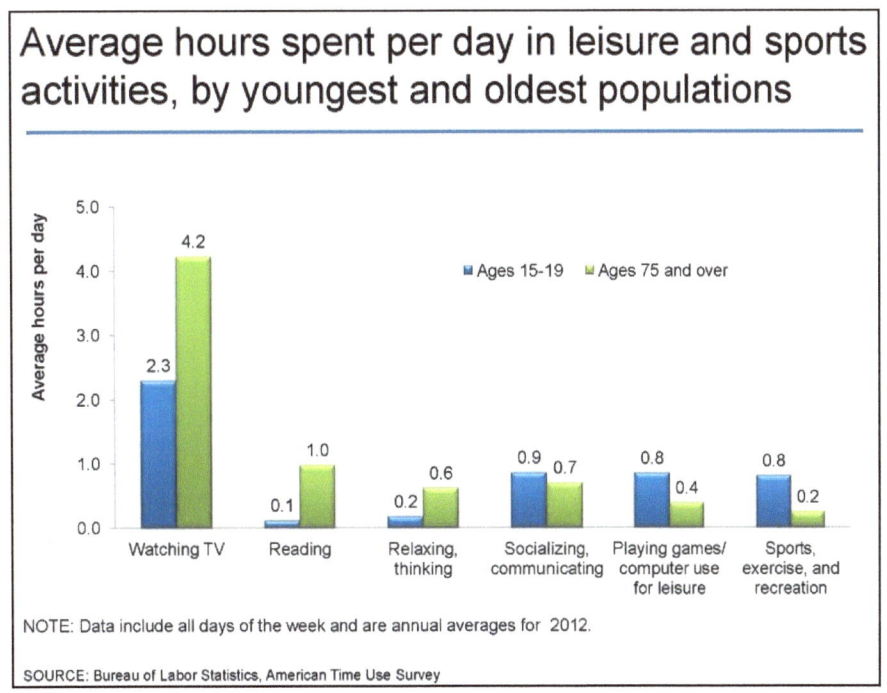

Source: U.S. Bureau of Labor Statistics

This data might suggest that reading is on the way out, but the latest NEA (National Endowment for the Arts) data shows that over half of Americans (54.5%) read at least one book in 2012, down only slightly from the 56.6% recorded in its 2002 report.

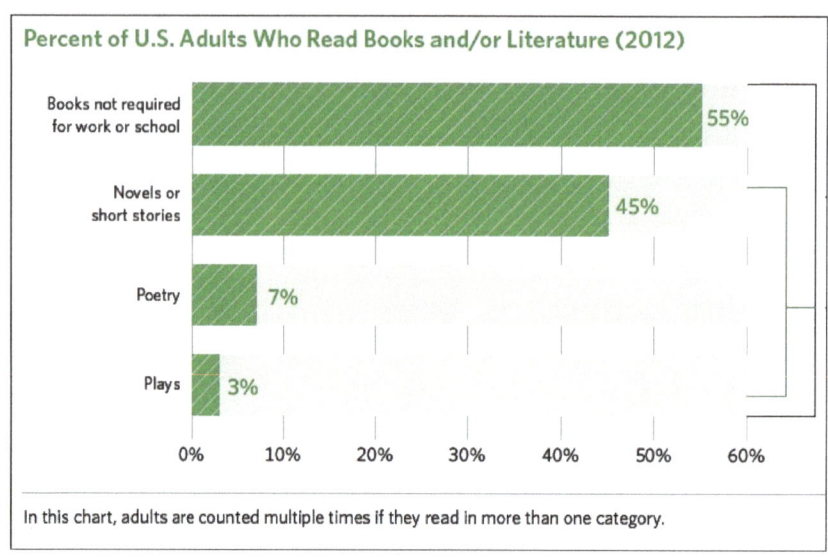

Source: National Endowment for the Arts (NEA)

[A Pew report](#) included figures from polls going back to 1978. While the number of people who don't read books increased, the 2011 Pew figures show that 49% of American read six or more books in the previous year. Enthusiasm for reading varies by race/ethnicity, income and level of education. Last year U.S. population growth [dropped to 0.7%](#), the lowest level since the Great Depression. [Population-growth demographic analysis](#) shows that U.S. publishers can't expect net new book readers to enter the market. Growth will come either from selling more books to existing readers or from international markets.

Extrapolating from the [Pew data](#) suggests that those who read eleven or more books per year account for as many as 85% of total books sold.

Book reading trends over time
% of adults (age 18+) who say they have read this number of books in the past 12 months

	Pew Internet 12/2011	Gallup 5/2005	Gallup 12/2001	Gallup 9/1999	Gallup 12/1990	Gallup 7/1978
None	19%	16%	13%	13%	16%	8%
1-5 books	32	38	38	30	32	29
6-10 books	15	14	16	16	15	17
11-50 books	26	25	23	31	27	29
>50 books	5	6	8	7	7	13
Don't know - refused	3	1	1	2	3	4
Mean	17	14.2	14.5	17	11	n/a
Median	8	5	5	7	6	n/a

Source: Pew Research Center Internet & American Life Project

Another chart in the same 2012 survey shows that the youngest readers are at the head of the reading class.

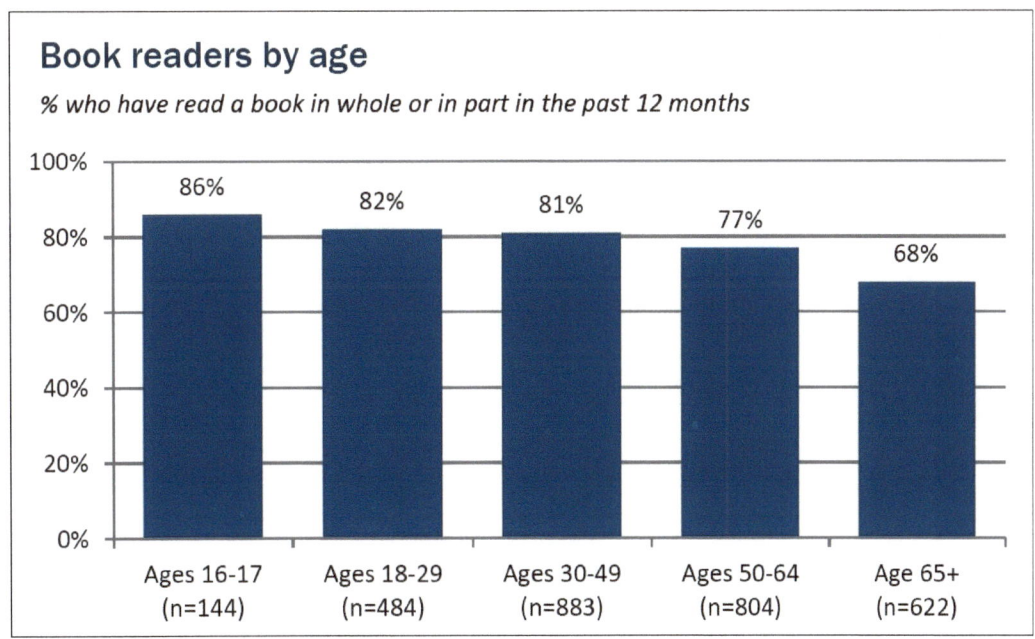

Source: Pew Research Center Internet & American Life Project

TAKEAWAYS FOR PUBLISHERS

People still read. Lots. Young people in particular. But they do other things, like watch TV and play games, even more. The takeaway for mobile marketers is that online is the way to reach the most readers—or at least through a screen.

ENGLISH EVERYWHERE

The chart below brings home an important point: North America is not the world leader in mobile subscriptions.

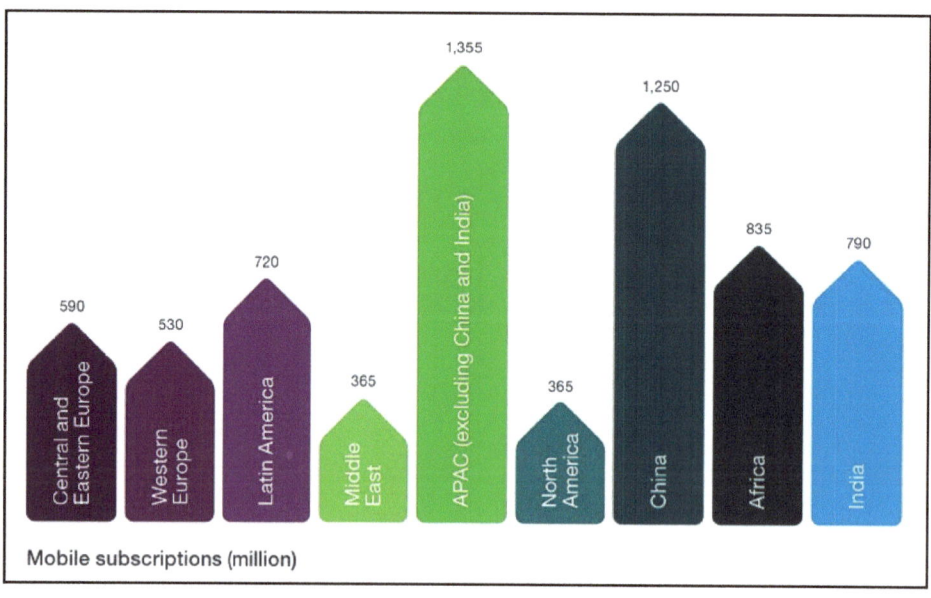

Source: Ericsson Mobility Report, June, 2014

But mobile subscriptions aren't the most revealing metric. Language is more important, and English dominates across populations and across the publishing industry.

Based on statistics [compiled by the British Council](#):

- English is spoken as a first language by around 375 million and as a second language by an additional 375 million speakers in the world.

- Around 750 million people speak English as a foreign language (where English is not spoken as a first or second language).

- One out of four of the world's population speaks English to some level of competence, and demand from the other three-quarters is increasing.

[Some 2 billion people worldwide](#) are learning English.
(See following chart.)

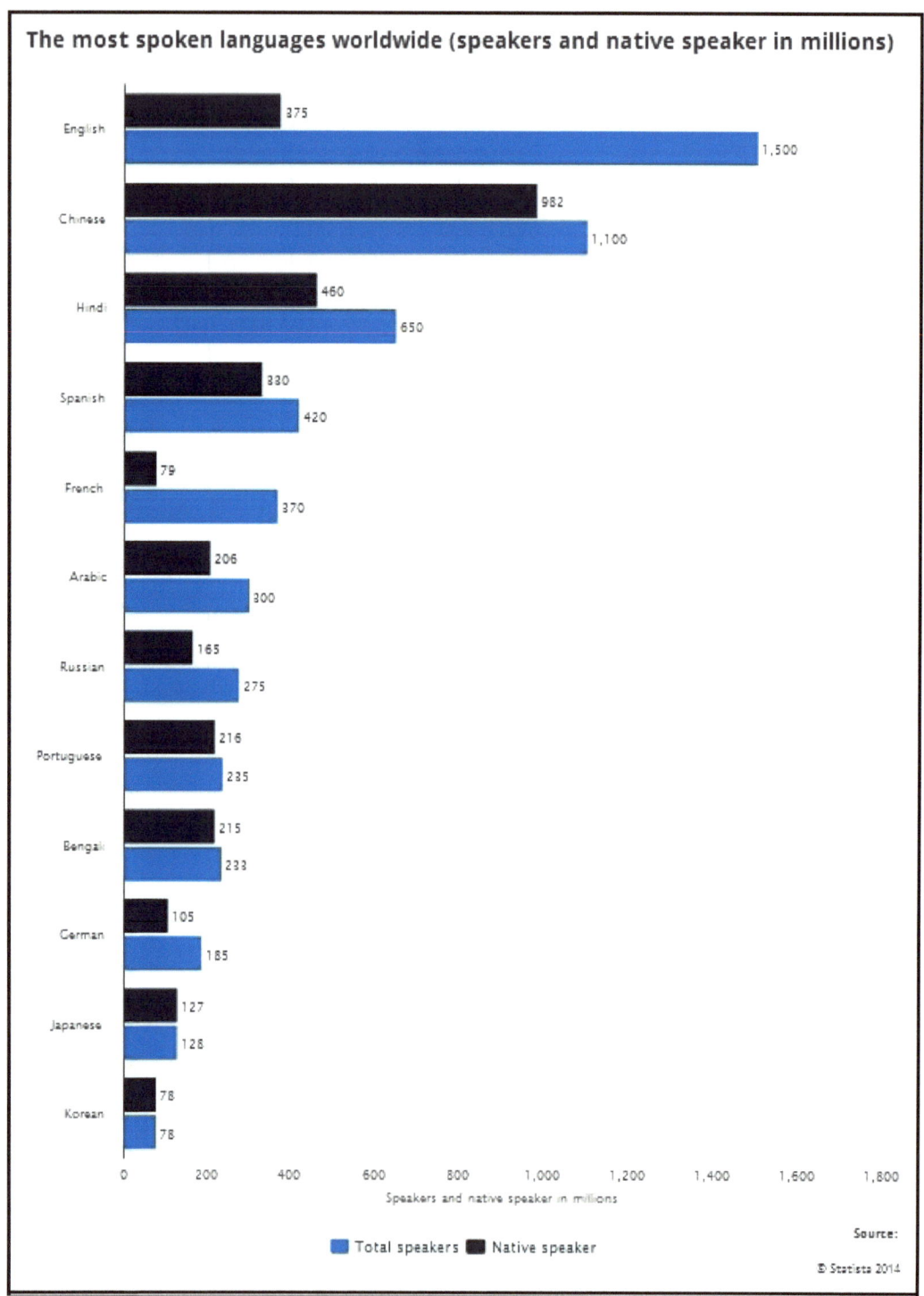

Source: Statista

Data from the 2013 edition of Education First's English Proficiency Index offers publishers a means to prioritize marketing of English publications based on each country's degree of English proficiency.

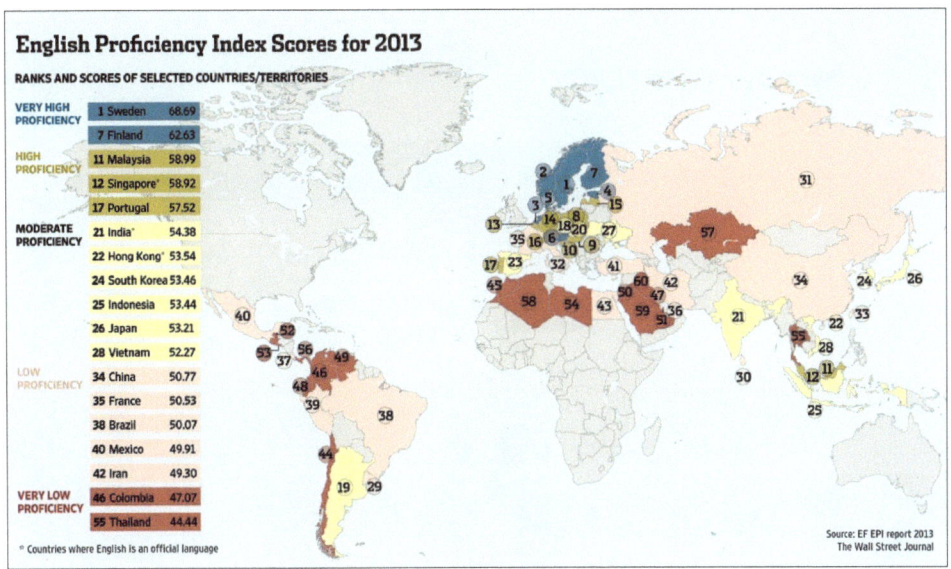

Source: The Wall Street Journal

TAKEAWAYS FOR PUBLISHERS

Publishers fearing a stagnating book market in the U.S. and UK can take heart that ebooks and e-commerce offer access to an enormous worldwide market of English speakers and English learners. Pricing is an issue in many of the less developed countries. Mobile strategies must be international in scope.

BOOK BUYERS ARE ONLINE

The largest channel for book buying—of digital and physical combined—is online. Bricks-and-mortar sales divide into six smaller channels.

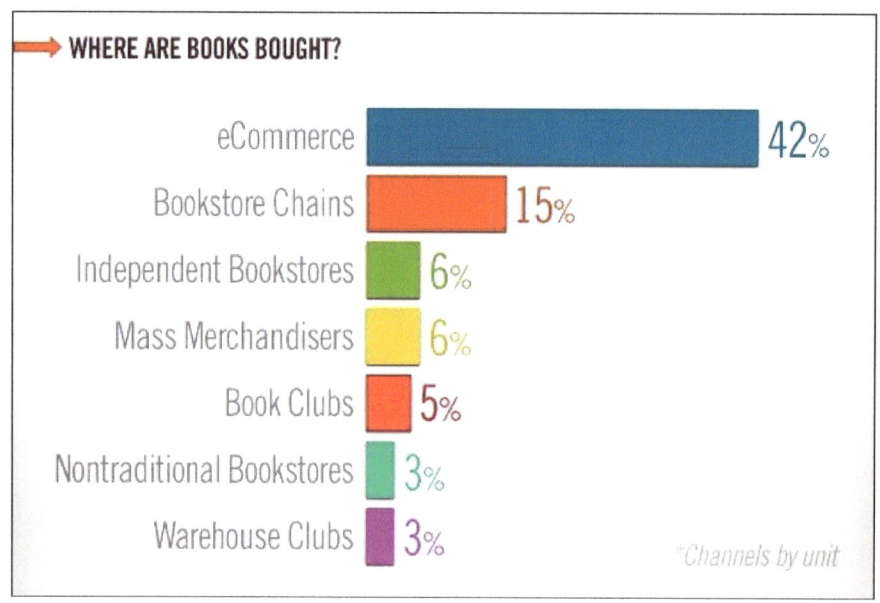

Source: Bowker U.S. Book Consumer Demographics & Buying Behaviors Review, 2013

Measuring just ebook sales, estimates place Amazon at 65% of the U.S. market and 79% in the UK. According to George Packer, writing in the New Yorker, Apple and Barnes & Noble divide another 30% of U.S. ebook sales between them.

This is probably a loose estimate. BISG data suggests lower market shares for both Apple and Barnes & Noble.

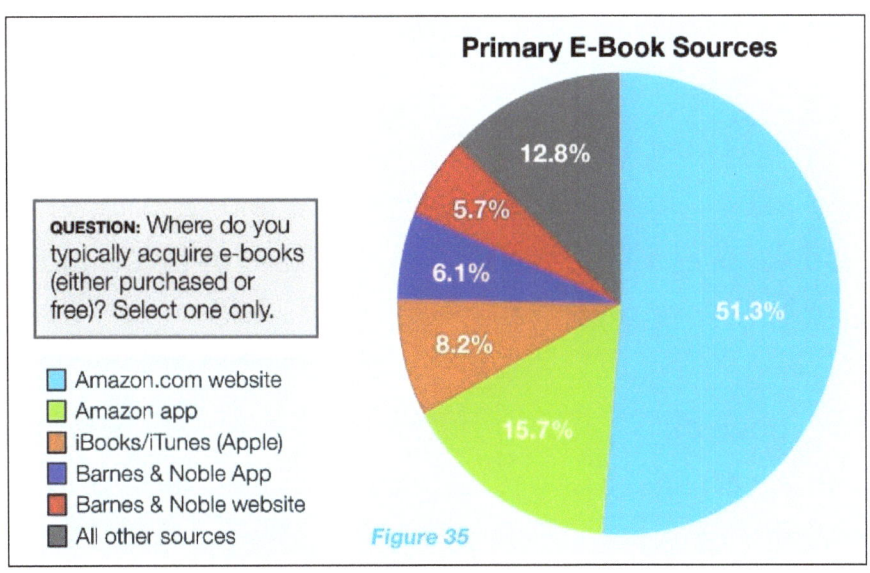

Source: BISG Consumer Attitudes Towards Ebook Reading, 2013

Ebooks command approximately 30% of books sold in the U.S., holding steady since mid-2013. Low ebook prices depress the dollar volume to less than half the unit volume.

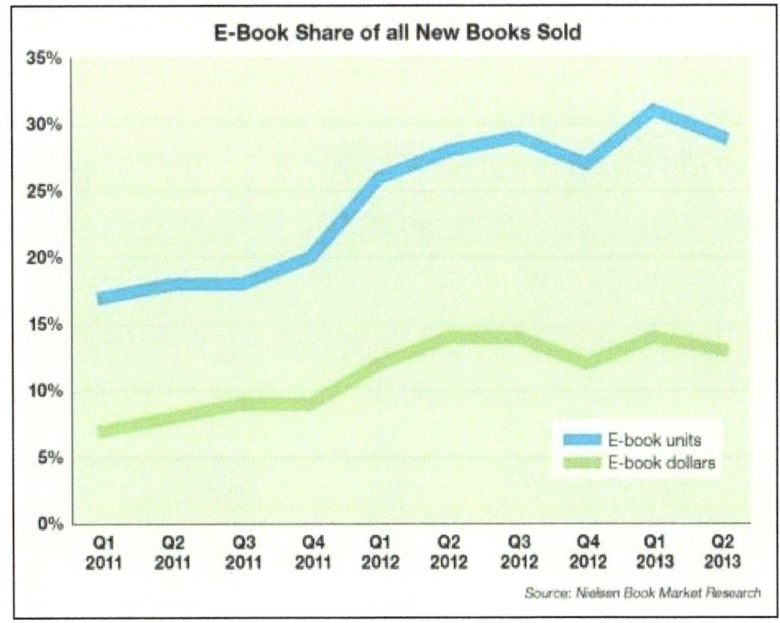

Source: Nielsen Book Market Research

TAKEAWAYS FOR PUBLISHERS

Book buying is now overwhelmingly online. It's the choice of twice as many people as those who choose chain and independent retail bookstores. The focus for marketers must start with e-tailers, with Amazon chief among them.

Amazon's power is no secret, but the full extent of its book retail dominance can still surprise. Its strength in selling print books undermines both chain and retail bookstores directly. With two-thirds of the U.S. retail share for ebooks, there's no clear No. 2 competing head-to-head with Amazon.

The Amazon-Hachette dispute has settled without a clear winner. Closer involvement and friendly cooperation with Amazon is the single most important tactic for a publisher to implement. Can any company refuse to devote full attention to its largest customer?

As of this writing, U.S. ebook sales have been hovering between 25% and 30% of total book sales for over a year. Growth has stalled. No one knows whether a 30% ebook market share is the new norm. It may just signal a pause as ebook formats become more appealing, prices drop or digital rights management (DRM) disappears.

QUANTIFYING E-READING DEVICES

At BookExpo America (BEA) 2014 Nielsen released data on device ownership among U.S. book buyers. While the percentage of households with e-readers is declining, the two charts below demonstrate the ongoing importance of e-readers to publishers.

Another significant point concealed by ownership numbers is the popularity of Amazon's Kindle app on Apple's devices. The download figures are hidden, but the Kindle app has twice as many reviews as iBooks on the iTunes store. (The current version of the Kindle app has significantly more positive reviews than iBooks.)

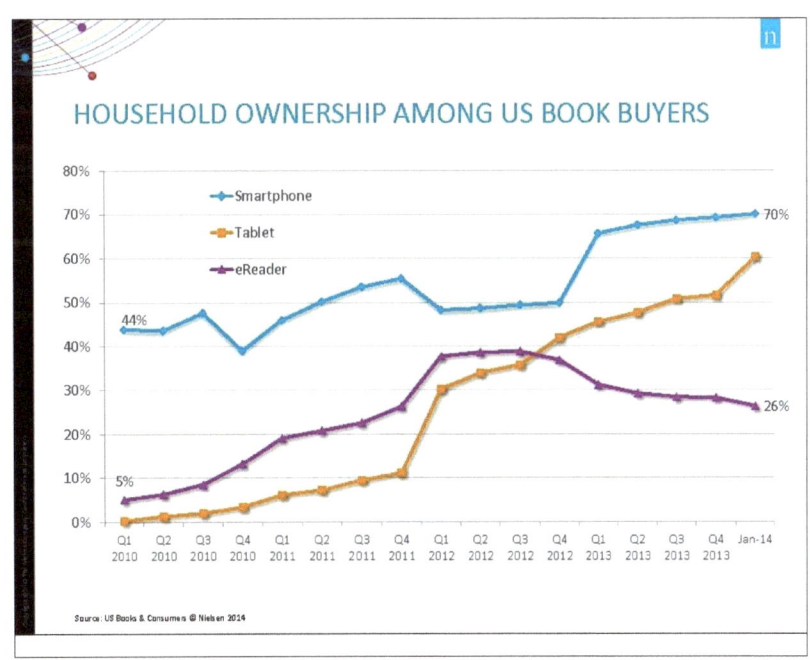

Source: Nielsen Book Market Research

An [October 2013 report from the Book Industry Study Group (BISG)](#) offers a slightly different view of device ownership among "adults who have said they read ebooks." The chart below illustrates the split between ownership of e-readers and tablets. E-readers, both Amazon's Kindle & Barnes & Noble's NOOK, appear to total about 48% (vs. 26% in the Nielsen data above). The five different tablets were owned between them by about 75% of respondents (vs. 60% in the Nielsen data).

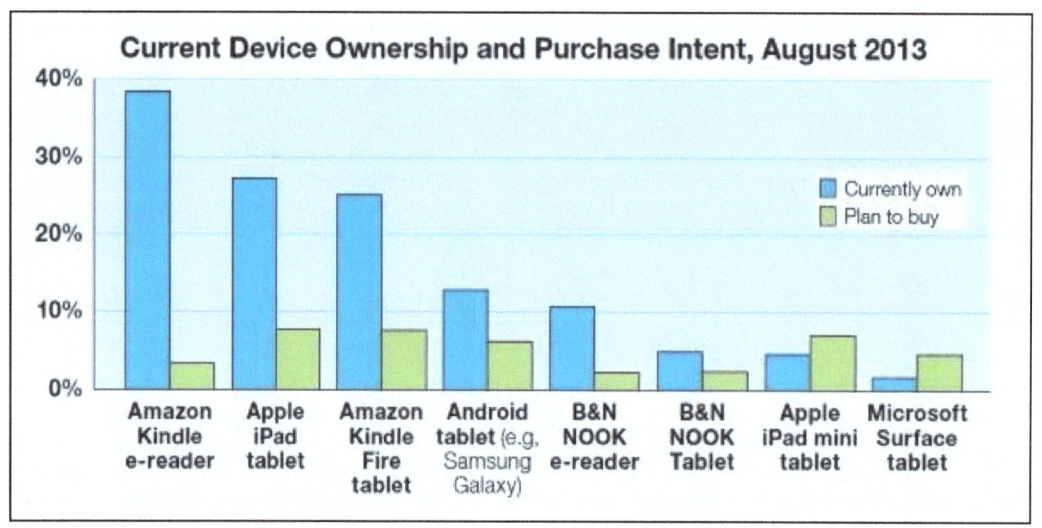

Source: Nielsen Book Market Research

Tablets are the top mobile device for ebook purchases, followed closely by e-readers. Smartphones represent a small percentage of the total (online print purchases aren't surveyed).

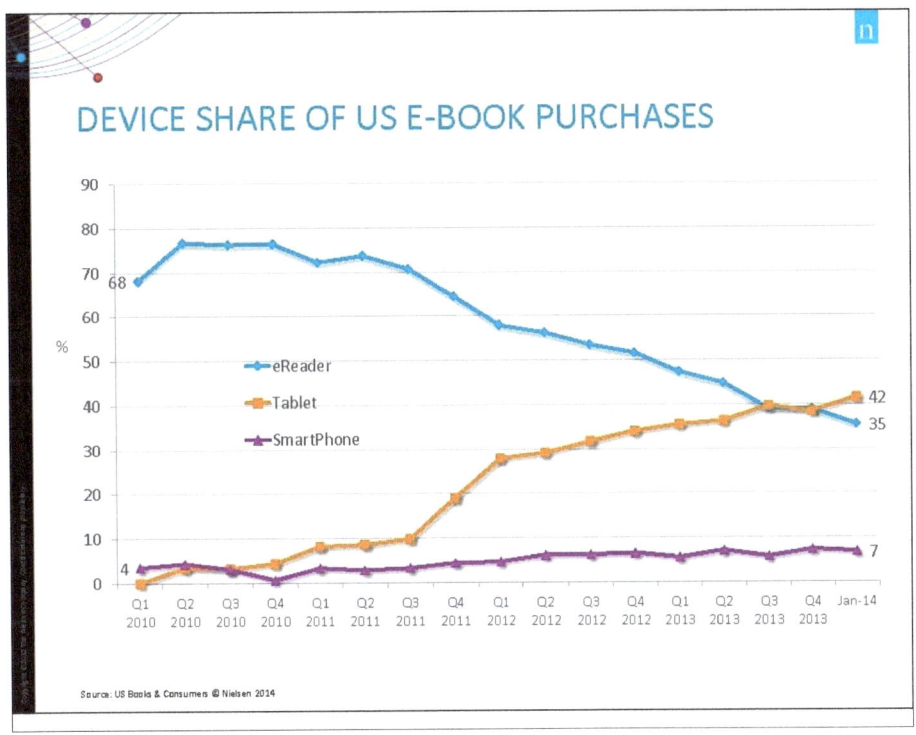

Source: Nielsen Book Market Research

In January 2014 the Pew Research Center's Internet and American Life Project published a useful report, *E-Reading Rises as Device Ownership Jumps*. It broadly examines ebook readership as well as readership by device. The chart below compares the use of different devices specifically as e-readers. The responses are limited just to those who own each device.

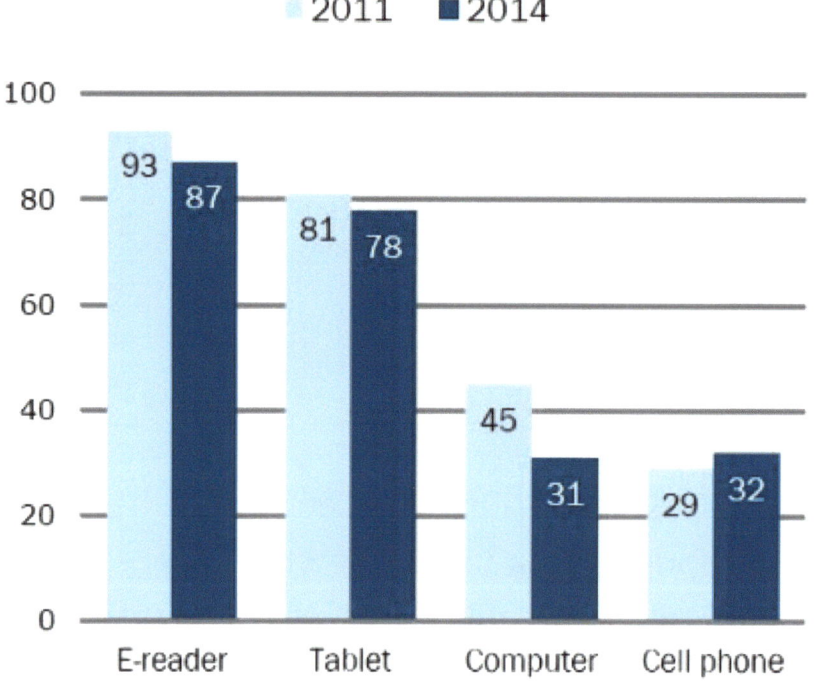

Source: Pew Research Center Internet Project

The numbers are high because the timeframe for the question is a full year. What Pew failed to do with this analysis was tabulate the *frequency of use* for each device (data available in the later section of the report). Limiting the chart above just to those who use the device *every day* or a *few times a week* (leaving out usage of just a few times a month or less often), the data paints a different picture:

Frequency of Use for Each Device	
E-reader	53%
Tablet	31%
Computer	9%
Cell phone	12%

Source: Author, Pew Research Center Internet Project

Owners of personal computers and cell phones use each of them frequently to read ebooks, roughly 10% of the time. Though twice as many book-buying households own tablets as own e-readers, the latter are nearly twice as popular for frequent ebook reading. Data from the RJI Mobile Media News Consumption Survey finds an average of 14% of smartphone owners use them to read books, versus 41% using tablets for reading, three times greater than on smartphones.

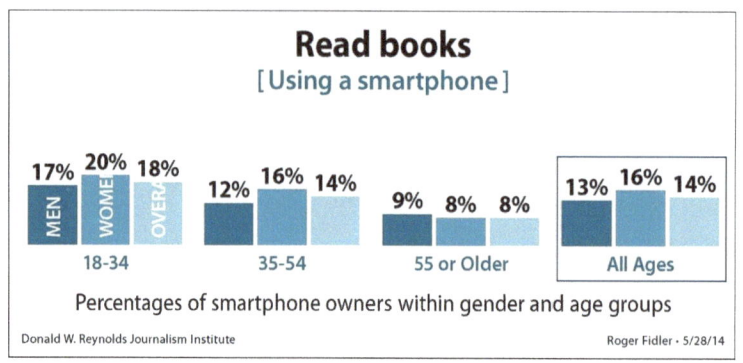

Source: Donald W. Reynolds Journalism Institute

TAKEAWAYS FOR PUBLISHERS

Different devices engender different consumer behavior. For mobile marketing, the devil's in the details. Tablets are increasing their hold while smartphones, although owned by 70% of readers, aren't much used for ebook reading or ebook buying.

Though now in a slow decline, the large installed base of dedicated e-readers (estimated at roughly 50 million in the U.S., and perhaps double that number worldwide) remains a top source for ebook purchases and reading. E-readers provide some degree of web access and some social features, but the major play for publishers to e-reader owners is selling lots of additional titles to these devoted book readers.

Also important to keep in mind is that there are about twice as many smartphone owners as there are tablet owners. Some 95% of U.S. households own PCs. The total number of readers per device skews differently than the use frequency.

WHAT DO THE CHARTS TELL US?

- Mobile has exploded—really exploded. There are 175 million smartphone users in the U.S.; 65% of the YA and adult population. Tablet ownership is roughly half that, at 34%.

- PCs remain more important than mobile devices for most uses (except ebook reading). But just about *everyone* owns a PC.

- In smartphones, the contest is between Apple and the various vendors of Android phones. Android is quickly gaining market share, although iPhone owners are a devoted bunch. They're not going away.

- In tablets, Apple continues to dominate the U.S. market. It has over half of the installed base. More importantly, iPad users use their tablets far longer each day than the competition. They also spend more, both on apps and for shopping.

- Tablets and smartphones are shopping machines, although as much as 90% of e-commerce originates on PCs.

- Mobile users favor apps over the mobile web, and by a large margin. Apple's iOS and Google's Android each offer 1.2 million different apps. A small handful of apps command the bulk of user engagement—gaming, social media and texting apps garner over half of users' time.

- Still, the average mobile user spends as much as 30 minutes a day on the mobile web.

- Watching TV remains the top leisure activity for the average American (2.8 hours per day).

- Despite all claims to the contrary, American are still readers and are reading as much as ever. Half of Americans read six or more books a year (and 5% read over 50 books a year). Heavy readers account for perhaps 85% of books sold. The heaviest readers may be the youngest.

- Publishers mostly underestimate the total English-speaking audience for their books. English is the first or second language for 750 million people and a foreign language for another 75 million. An even larger group, 2 billion, is learning English. Ebooks online make foreign customers more accessible than ever before, although U.S. ebook pricing leaves many books out of reach in less-developed countries.

- Nearly half of book buying originates online. Chain and independent bookstores account for only half of that percentage. Ebook buying, upwards of 30% of unit sales, is (obviously) 100% online. Amazon has roughly two-thirds of the ebook market in the U.S. and four-fifths of the UK market.

- Book buyers own lots of smartphones, tablets and e-readers. E-readers are used frequently by half of readers; tablets by a third; cell phones and PCs about 10% each. Another survey (which didn't include e-readers) found that people were three times more likely to read a book on a tablet than on a smartphone.

- But e-readers remain one of the top sources for ebook purchases, tied with tablets.

CHAPTER 2
MOBILE STRATEGIES FOR CONTENT

Content is the lynchpin of any publisher's mobile strategy. The variety of mobile devices demands different approaches to designing and formatting content.

This chapter focuses just on the ways in which content influences a publisher's mobile *strategy*. The following chapter, Chapter 3, *Tools for Building Ebooks and Apps*, adds technical details for selecting formats and showcasing content. Chapter 4, *Mobile Marketing Strategies,* drills down on marketing strategies and tactics. Inevitably, there is some overlap and these three chapters are closely intertwined.

THE CONTAINER AND THE BOOK

Publishing has traditionally treated the manuscript as sacrosanct and so built the print book "container" around an author's words.

Manuscript → Print Book

Publishers follow the same path with ebooks, plus an extra step: they usually generate the ebook file directly from the Adobe InDesign file or the PDF used for the print version.

Manuscript → InDesign/PDF file for Print Book → Ebook

There are obvious drawbacks to automatically calling on InDesign/PDF files for ebooks. Too many ebooks have blank pages, half-title pages and copyright pages at the front of the book. It was a tradition in printed books, for legal and aesthetic reasons. Best practices today for ebooks call for moving publication and copyright information to the back of the book. Readers want to get right to the story.

THE DIGITAL CONTENT DECISION

The print format path used to be so wonderfully simple. Start with hardcover. Then move to trade paperback or directly to mass-market paperback (or sometimes trade and then mass-market paperback). There were minor variations but few choices.

The path has changed. Simultaneous hardcover and ebook publication is the default. The second choice, increasingly popular, is simultaneous trade paperback and ebook publication. It can be followed by a less expensive trade paperback (or a mass-market paperback for much genre fiction).

A few years ago, publishers might stagger the ebook release for a month or more after the first print edition. That's rare these days. As of this writing none of the top twenty new print releases on Amazon lack for an e-book offering.

The choices made for digital editions can be complex. There's a broad range available but no clear decision path. Part of the problem is deciding which devices to target, e-readers, tablet and, increasingly, smartphones. Here's the digital menu:

1. **Basic ebook:** A simple ebook, with a modest number of fixed-format illustrations. This remains the publishing industry standard. Because most of these ebooks are read on dedicated e-readers, color highlights and color images are rendered in black and white.

2. **Enhanced ebook:** A colorful ebook, enriched with a variety of video, audio and (some) interactive features. These don't work well (or at all) on monochrome e-readers, but they shine on tablets (and sometimes on smartphones). Specialized enhanced ebooks are created with Apple's iBooks Author software or Inkling's Habitat. These programs arguably produce products closer to apps than to ebooks. They work on tablets and sometimes on smartphones. One vexing limitation is that ebooks created with iBooks Author can only be sold in the iBookstore.

3. **Book app:** Rethink the book and turn it into an app. Doing it right is expensive and the revenue model mostly unproven (with the exception of a healthy children's book market). This format works best on tablets and sometimes on smartphones.

	STANDARD EBOOK	ENHANCED EBOOK	APP
CAPABILITIES	Static words and images, creator has no control over quality of text and little control over how and where images appear.	Offers more features than a traditional ebook; can include audio, video, animation and interactivity.	An app can access all of the features of the device, including sounds, cameras, full audio & video, animations, interactivity and more.
HOW TO BUILD	Just run an MS Word doc or PDF through an EPUB or Mobi converter. Few skills required for a simple conversion.	The degree of difficulty is in direct relationship to the sophistication of the product. Requires experts.	Requires an experienced programmer.
PRICING EXPECTATIONS	Standard ebooks are usually cheaper than enhanced ebooks but more expensive than apps.	Depends on the sophistication of the ebook. Kids ebook as lower priced than adult titles.	Most book apps are in the $2.99-$4.99 range. Many are free with in-app ads or upselling.
SELLING LOCATION	All ebook stores worldwide, Amazon, Apple, Kobo, Barnes & Noble, etc.	There are subtle differences in the features supported by different ebook stores. Can be complex to match features to resellers.	The main app sellers are Apple and most Android (Google) resellers. Amazon is a smaller player for app sales.
DEVICE MOST OFTEN USED TO VIEW THIS	Dedicated e-readers, and increasingly on tablets and smartphones.	Kindle Fire, iPad.	iOS or Android smartphone or tablet.
WHERE IT LIVES ON CUSTOMER'S DEVICE	Inside a dedicated reader app, such as the Kindle, Nook or iBooks readers.	Inside a dedicated reader app, such as the Kindle, Nook or iBooks readers.	A standalone icon launched a discrete miniature software application.

Publishers long ago learned to fit content into the specific features and restraints of printed books. The range and flexibility of digital formats offer publishers a new set of choices to showcase a book's content.

One approach is to ask, Who am I trying to reach, and what device(s) do they use? Data to help guide those decisions can be found in Chapter 1 of this report. For example, dedicated e-readers are still the No. 1 device for reading ebooks. Where possible, content should be optimized first for their monochrome displays. Tablets, smartphones and PCs display full-color content. Apple iPads are more important than any other tablet brand, and Apple iPhones are more important than any other smartphone brand.

CONTENT STRATEGIES FOR ENHANCED EBOOKS

Back in the spring of 2011, Evan Schnittman, at the time Bloomsbury's director of sales and marketing, declared that enhanced ebooks were dead. "Enhanced will have an incredibly big future in education," he said, "but the idea of innovation in the narrative reading process is just a non-starter. I've been smug about this, and now I'm even smugger." Four years later, writing on *Digital Book World*, Peter Costanzo noted that, for a variety of reasons, Evan Schnittman was mostly right.

Amazon doesn't list "enhanced ebooks" as a category. Searching "enhanced ebooks" on the Kindle store returns only 163 results, including a handful from a publisher called "Enhanced Ebooks."

It's instructive to look at the available enhanced ebooks on Barnes & Noble and Amazon. There are 2,150 results for "NOOK Books Enhanced" (out of 3,934,005 results for "NOOK books"). As usual, some books of questionable quality slip into the mix—perhaps best indicated by the inclusion of the 85-megabyte "An Interactive Biography of James Dean for Kids (Enhanced Edition)."

This multi-megabyte title also illustrates a recurring problem of enhanced ebooks and apps: Adding video rapidly bloats the file size. Amazon charges authors 15¢ per megabyte against each customer ebook download. The charges for large files can exceed the revenue from the book. And customers become frustrated downloading large files to mobile devices.

A broad rule for enhanced ebooks: high-profile titles can sometimes bring in incremental revenue through enhanced versions. For all others, caution is required.

CONTENT STRATEGIES FOR APPS

Can publishers convert print books into apps and find new customers? Books are two-dimensional and static. Apps are multi-dimensional and interactive. Books gain little value when translated directly into an app.

On the other hand, the market for children's apps is now clearly established. Many are based on classic children's books. And there's a lot of innovation in the category.

Many award-winning so-called "book apps" are mostly built from scratch. They resemble software more than they do books, and so demand the skills and the vision of software engineers and digital entrepreneurs.

Publishers rely on "reader apps" to trigger multimedia, interactivity and other special properties built into enhanced ebooks. The [features of the Kindle reading app](#) are well known. Third-party reader apps, like [Calibre](#) or [Lexcycle Stanza](#), can be more flexible and sometimes more powerful. The DRM built into paid ebooks makes it impossible to use these readers without illegally unlocking the file. Publishers mainly work within these DRM constraints.

A GLIMPSE AT BOOK APPS

Kirkus is the most respected source of professional reviews of book apps. It's Best Book Apps of 2013 records forty top apps reviewed in 2013. Tellingly, only seven target the adult market; the rest are kid's books. The 2014 list includes five adult apps out of 25 total.

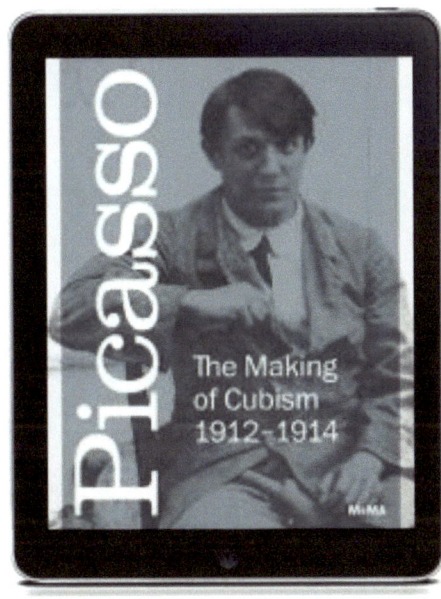

It's worth tracking Kirkus's app reviews. A recent and positive review (for other than a children's app) is *Picasso: The Making of Cubism 1912–1914*, developed by MoMA, The (New York) Museum of Modern Art. The review is largely positive for this $25 app (that weighs in at 750 megabytes).

THE MOST POPULAR APPLE AND ANDROID APPS

Publishers regularly scan best-seller lists to find out what's selling like hotcakes, what's trending and what's failing. The best-sellers lists for apps provide an equivalent value. Best-seller lists for books are subdivided by fiction/nonfiction and hardbound/paperback. App listings feature different divisions. The two major platforms, iOS and Android, each have separate charts. Within each platform both free and paid apps are recorded.

There's not a book to be found in the top 100 free apps and top 100 paid apps on the Apple iTunes App Store. Games dominate. Likewise among the free apps and paid apps on Android.

Source: King.com Ltd.

The most popular book apps on the iTunes App Store and the Google Play store are free religious books—versions of the Bible, the Quran, etc.—most offered in several languages. The next largest category are free ebook reader software. Brand names like Kindle and Kobo mingle with the more numerous third-party reader apps (such as the Aldiko Book Reader and the Moon+ Reader). Other popular categories are dictionaries (including the Online Cree Dictionary, with a 4.6/5 rating) and collections of free ebooks (such as Oodles's 50,000 Free Ebooks and Reader).

The most successful free apps are supported by third-party advertising within the app and/or by encouraging users to upgrade to a premium paid version.

In the paid category on Android, standalone book titles enter the best-seller list, including Dr. Seuss books like *The Cat in the*

Hat and Sandra Boynton's popular titles such as *The Going to Bed Book*. Nearly all of the best-selling books are children's titles. [On the Apple store](#) a few inspirational and occult tiles also make the list.

Children's book apps are usually spin-offs from other children's media, whether film, TV or books. Some are just generic titles such as "This Little Piggy" or "Classic Stories for Young Readers." Some are created as original apps, such as "[The Fantastic Flying Books of Mr. Morris Lessmore](#)," "[Even Monsters Get Sick](#)" and "[Midnight Feast](#)."

A handful of websites offer more detailed and easier-to-access best-seller charts:

- [App Annie](#) is the gold standard for app best-seller listings. Beyond the iOS/Android and free/paid charts, App Annie mines sales for Windows Phone and for Amazon as well as apps for Mac and Windows PCs.

- [TopAppCharts](#) has a homemade feel to its interface but provides a useful counterpoint to App Annie's numbers.

- [AppCrawlr: The App Discovery Engine](#) provides a fast and easy way to discover book-related apps.

CONCLUSION

Making the best choices for formatting and distributing digital content demands a comprehensive appreciation of devices, software and users. While EPUB remains the industry's [standards-based ebook format](), e-tailers provide varying feature support. Publishers are challenged and users frustrated because the specifics constantly change.

Apps are on track to being the most important way for publishers to interact with mobile users. This chapter introduced apps for publishing. The next chapter outlines the best approaches to building ebooks and apps, while the following chapter explores mobile marketing strategies.

CHAPTER 3
TOOLS FOR BUILDING EBOOKS AND APPS

Delivering content in digital formats is still demanding for book publishers. Challenges persist both in file formats and in differing screen displays.

Multiple file formats plague ebook delivery. While EPUB and Mobi are the two most popular formats, EPUB has two variants in use and Mobi has a successor format called Amazon KF8.

Publishers are now comfortable creating just text-only ebooks. The degree of difficulty rises when images are added to the text, (and soon after with audio and video).

Digital displays come in different sizes, [aspect ratios](#) and both in monochrome and in color.

These challenges affect websites, ebooks, enhanced ebooks and apps, though each in different ways.

ENHANCED EBOOKS

The previous chapter described the market challenges surrounding enhanced ebooks. The opportunity for trade publishers of adult books remains slight, though some publishers have cracked the code.

Enhanced ebooks exasperate digital publishers. There's not even a widely accepted definition for the term. Broadly speaking, enhanced ebooks add audio, video and interactive features to a book's text. But some publishers consider the addition of a bunch of photographs to be a defined enhancement.

Enhanced ebooks can mean any and all of the following:

- An ebook created using the EPUB 3 standard, which supports audio, video, animation and interactive content. Most e-reading software has limited support for EPUB3 (see chart below). E-readers that accept EPUB3 files usually don't support all of its file features. O'Reilly Media's Sanders Kleinfeld provided a detailed analysis of the long-range opportunities inherent in the EPUB 3 format.

- Amazon uses a different enhanced ebook standard called KF8, which is less robust than the EPUB 3 specification, forcing publishers to optimize their ebook files separately for sale on Amazon.com.

- Ebooks created using Apple iBooks Author output to the Apple iBooks format — and can be sold only through Apple.

- Inkling's standalone enhanced ebook publishing platform called Habitat. Inkling explains that "the content you'll build is HTML5, and Habitat lets you instantly build your content to fully standards-compliant EPUB 3."

This table from eBook Architects illustrates the mess found at the intersection of file formats and most digital readers. (Keep in mind that the details change frequently.)

	Apple	Amazon	B&N	Kobo	Sony	Google
Format	ePub2/ePub3	KF8	NOOK Kids	ePub3	ePub3	ePub3
Narration	✓	✗	✓	✓	✗	✗
Narration Text Highlighting	✓	✗	✗	✗	✗	✗
Region/Text Magnification	✗	✓	✓	✗	✗	✗
Embedded Audio/Video	✓	✗*	✗	✓	✗	✗
Background Music	✓	✗	✗	✗	✗	✗
Animations	✓	✗	✗	✗	✗	✗
Interactive Elements	✓	✗	✗	✗	✗	✗

Source: eBook Architects Enhanced Ebook Examples

ENHANCED EBOOK EXAMPLES

- Apple has an iBooks Author Gallery illustrating the range of features available in the software.

- Blurb specializes in illustrated books, primarily photo books. The company offers a simple PDF conversion tool to create enhanced ebooks for the Apple iBookstore (output as iBooks for iPad format). An Enhanced Ebook Gallery shows the range of titles created on Blurb.

- Each title in the Inkling Store includes a free sample. The Habitat User Guide explains the ins and outs of creating Inkling ebooks.

APP DEVELOPMENT

Very few book publishers develop apps in-house; most use contractors. Managing the many variables that go into designing and coding an app demands new skills, in fact a new team. And it's a constant chore to keep an app up to date on two or more platforms (usually iOS and Android, but sometimes Windows and/or Blackberry as well). Some apps are targeted just for smartphones, others for tablets and some for both.

Budgeting the initial cost of an app can be treacherous. Costs can range from $5,000 to $250,000 depending on an equally broad range of factors. Publishers have a hard time making these expensive decisions internally and so it's essential to find an experienced contractor. They in turn select the app development agency and supervise the building and delivery of the product.

Digital Book World published a detailed case study on app creation with a focus on children's apps. The study describes how

Wasabi Productions created "Lazy Larry Lizard," its first app, and looks also at the development of "Gorilla Band," its second app.

PRODUCTION PARTNERS

Most publishers work with outside production partners rather than building ebook and app production skills in-house. Audio/video and interactive features demand skilled technicians. Here are some of the industry's most respected production services. Some focus exclusively on ebook production while others can handle apps as well. URLs are linked to company names.

APTARA

From their website: "A digital publishing leader for twenty-five years, Aptara excels in getting engaging digital content products to digital consumers faster and more cost-effectively. Aptara's wide-ranging subject matter experts deploy smart content technologies across every aspect of production—and produce the entire spectrum of digital end products, including ebooks, apps, websites, and eMagazines."

CODEMANTRA

From their website: "codeMantra is one of the leading providers of composition and conversion services, specializing in XML-first workflows for highly complex content creation, design, and distribution." Global distribution services include automated distribution of files and metadata plus file validation and compliance.

EBOOK ARCHITECTS

From their website: "eBook Architects, a service of Firebrand Technologies, works with authors and publishers of all sizes, designing high-quality ebooks for the Kindle, iPad, NOOK, and other devices. Our team develops the best in complex ebooks, including cookbooks, poetry, Bibles, textbooks, scientific and technical manuals, journals, chess manuals, and more.

IMPELSYS

From their website: "Over the years, Impelsys has developed successful ebook strategies for a number of leading publishers worldwide. Given our knack for technology and our intuitive sense for amazing user experience, we build apps that offer a delightful reading experience to your readers."

INTEGRA

Integra is one of the leading digital content services companies providing content enrichment and learning transformation services to publishers and educational institutions while also providing workplace learning and development solutions for enterprises.

Headquartered in Pondicherry, India, Integra has its global service delivery centers in India, Japan and the US besides providing project management & editorial support out of UK, Spain and Italy. Integra is the principal sponsor of this report. For more information, visit www.integra.co.in.

ONLINE APP TOOLS

There are dozens of web-based services offering "free" app creation, often supplemented with premium-priced assistance for more complex apps. The price kicks in as a monthly fee for hosting the app, with most around $20–$100 per month. Still, these platforms provide a much lower-cost app build, and possibly an appropriately cautious way to launch an app publishing program.

Here's a selection of the tools and services available, chosen to provide a range of services while favoring lower-cost platforms.

APPY PIE

Appy Pie lets you build an Android app for free; apps for Apple's iOS cost extra. For $19/month you can remove the "relevant" ads. The app building tools are drag and drop: no coding skills are required. Preview the HTML5 version of the app for this book here.

APPMAKR

From their website: "AppMakr is a do-it-yourself app creation platform that lets anyone make your own iPhone apps, Android apps and HTML5 mobile formatted websites—with no coding required." The monthly cost is only $9. The company is now part of Infinite Monkeys, which claims that 12% of app developers use its software.

APPSBAR

Appsbar gallery of apps includes many book apps. It offers a custom-built module specifically for books and authors. Appsbar is free, but as one reviewer noted, "If you are on a budget and need a community app then this is probably OK, but for serious commercial use I do not think this is up to the standard of other applications."

APPSME

From their website: "Appsme is an easy-to-use website that enables anyone to build a mobile app for their business… It's a simple 3-step process and the app will work on iPhones, Android phones and all other phones." The cost to publish on all major platforms is $40/month.

PAPERTRELL

Papertrell's offering is specific to book publishing. From their website: "A scalable and cost effective solution for publishers to re-purpose books as apps… specifically designed to help publishers, writers and content owners to package books as interactive apps that run on multiple devices." Pricing starts at $20/month. The company offers one-off services including design, conversion and marketing priced at between $500 and $1,000 per app.

THEAPPBUILDER

TheAppBuilder differentiates itself from the other app platforms not simply as the "world's leading mobile app platform." Their focus is "enterprise mobile apps" —they advise that their build-it-yourself tools are for "advanced users only." For inexperienced app creators they offer to build the app for you. Pricing is not disclosed online.

APP SALES REPORTING

After publishing an app the next step is to keep track of downloads and sales figures. Here are two popular services:

APP ANNIE

After raising [nearly $100 million in venture capital funding](#) App Annie certainly appears to be the market leader in app analytics. Its dashboard "helps you track all your app publisher data, across iTunes, Google Play & Amazon. One dashboard for all your app revenue, downloads, ratings, reviews & rankings." There's no cost except for an advanced "enterprise" edition.

APPFIGURES

appFigures is a reporting platform for mobile app developers that brings together app store sales, ad data, worldwide reviews and hourly rank updates into an intuitive and informative reporting solution. Pricing is $9 per month plus $1.99 per app (the first five apps are free).

YOUR MOBILE WEB SITE

Mobile websites are different from sites designed for viewing on PC monitors. Tablets do a pretty good job of displaying PC-optimized sites; mobile phones do not. In most cases your site needs to be redesigned for mobile. Here are two services specializing in mobile websites:

PIXMOBI

Pixmobi is a sophisticated service to help port your existing website into a mobile version. The "Pro" version costs 99 €/month. Its Mobile Phone Emulator is a nifty tool that shows you just how bad your current site looks on a smartphone. (QuirkTools Screenfly is a simpler tool that lets you preview your website on different devices from mobile to large screen.)

DUDA

Duda creates mobile sites interactively using your existing site structure via an online interactive previewer. Very impressive. Pricing is $9/month.

CHAPTER 4
MOBILE MARKETING STRATEGIES

WHY MOBILE MARKETING MATTERS

Publishers can make a reasonable argument that their customers are not (primarily) on mobile. Sure, mobile is becoming more important. But mobile is not as important today as reviews and making sure the book is ranking highly on Amazon.

And indeed, there's some truth to what they're saying. But things are changing quickly. The stats in the first chapter of this report illustrate the scale and speed of those changes. In any case, marketing isn't about maintaining markets; it's about growing them. Mobile is where today's customers are headed and where tomorrow's customers already dwell.

START WITH STAFF

In a fall 2014 presentation at the FutureBook Conference, George Berkowski said, "A bunch of English majors sitting in a room are never going to build a great app." His words are harsh but they highlight the challenges publishers face in implementing mobile strategies.

[A report on mobile](#) published by the American Press Institute points to a key challenge in recruiting digital talent. Publishing companies aren't the only ones trying to adapt to mobile technology. Most industries—some able to afford top salaries and even stock options—are bidding for the limited pool of people with experience and expertise in mobile. Few publishers can compete.

Like other creative industries—think film and music—book publishing retains its allure at the intersection of culture and fame. It has little trouble hiring entry-level staff to work in the [third most expensive city in the world](#). Fifty-five years ago [the Two Cultures](#) isolated the technologists from the aesthetes. These days, technology immersion comes standard with a millennial hire. On balance, millennials can usually run rings around Gen X and the remaining baby boomers on staff when it comes to technological prowess.

But although millennials are digital natives, are they publishing marketers? They might have the skillset, but don't yet have the experience.

Mobile marketing requires a leader who can articulate a compelling technology strategy and keep it on course. This is the most vexing issue for publishers, and there is not an easy answer.

Mobile won't succeed without a top-level commitment at the company. That's because a mobile program will cost more than was budgeted, take longer to complete than planned, and will initially deliver poorer results than expected. If the chief executive of the company isn't willing to weather a few losses the program won't have a chance to fly.

A mobile strategy must be explicit and fully documented. A common problem when implementing new technology programs is losing focus and then wandering off course.

Networking with colleagues at industry events helps marketers stay current. Mobile tech conferences such as the [Mobile Media Summit](#) and the [Mobile Marketing Strategies Summit](#) offer broad perspectives on mobile strategies. Conferences focused on digital strategies for magazine and newspaper publishers land closer to home. The top book industry conference is [Digital Book World's annual January event](#).

THE MOBILE MINDSET

There's a useful term from science fiction/computer science that helps characterize the mobile mindset: "grok." [One definition is](#): "to have an intuitive understanding of; to know something without having to think about it." When you dream in a foreign language, or can tell jokes in a foreign language, you grok it.

You won't grok mobile just by reading this report. You'll start to grok mobile when you wean yourself from your desktop computer and live your life on smartphones and tablets. You'll start to grok mobile when you shift *all* of your reading from print to digital. Grokking mobile means keeping in touch with friends and family via texting rather than email. Shopping mobile is grokking mobile.

To immerse themselves in the mobile universe, publishing staff require a tablet, a smartphone and an e-reader.

- Many of the best content apps are created just for Apple's iOS so the tablet should be an iPad.

- The smartphone could then be an Android phone in order to see how the other half lives (although, once again, publishing customers are more likely to be iPhone owners).

- Staff should also have access to a late model Android tablet.

- Without question, an Amazon Kindle is the e-reader choice.

MOBILE MARKETING PLANNING

Mobile marketers proclaim that [all marketing is now mobile](). Everything else, it's said, is a subset. Perhaps. For the next few years publishers are going to straddle the divide between traditional book marketing and other mobile initiatives. Here are a few steps to help move the plan along.

- Add a mobile strategy and project review to regular staff meetings. Set aside a block of time to brainstorm mobile strategies and assign responsibility for new mobile projects.

- Flip the table: Plan your next nonfiction publishing project for mobile platforms first. Imagine the book strictly as an app and then separately as an enhanced ebook. How would the content be enriched or compressed?

- Assign staff to review the company's backlist. Can they identify titles that might be suited to rebuilding as enhanced ebooks or apps?

And with mobile integrated into marketing it's also essential not to lose sight of the basics.

WHY DO READERS BUY BOOKS?

The factors influencing book buying were always varied. The chart below dates to 2002, before online sales moved the needle:

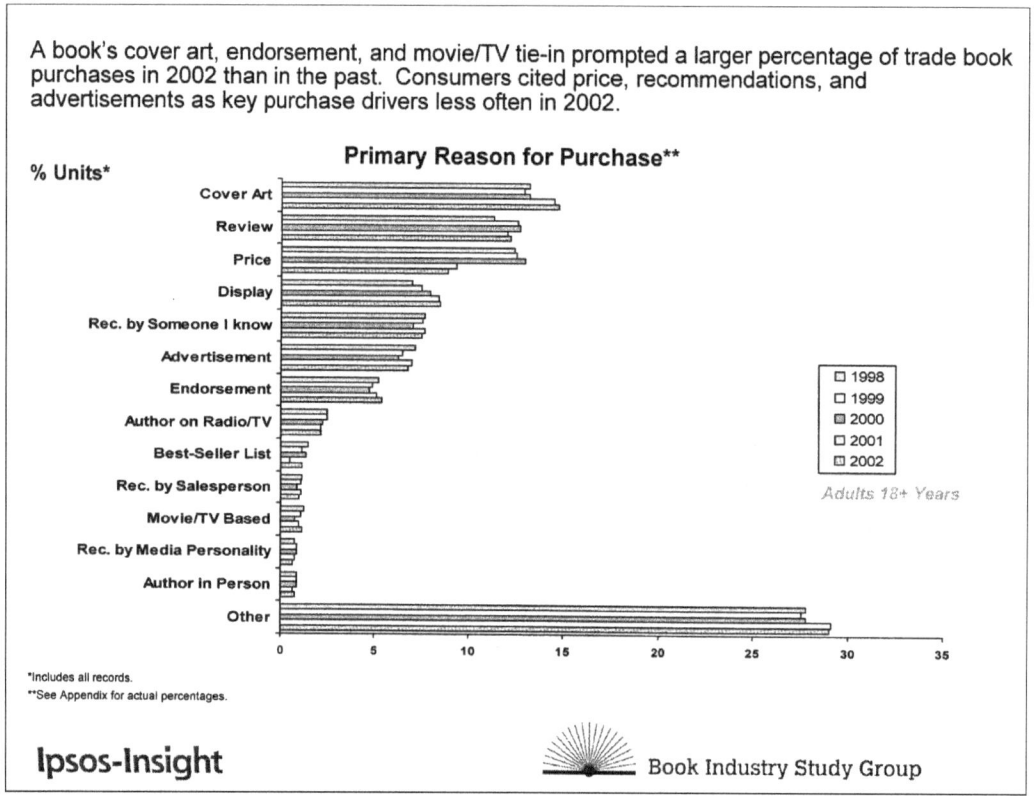

Source: Book Industry Study Group

Another pre-online buying survey, this one from the UK, details a variety of motivations.

Table 10.1 Purchase prompts for UK consumers (*source*: 2006 data from Book Facts Online)

Purchase prompt	Percentage of books bought
Saw in shop	35
Read other by author	14
Special information contained	13
Hobby information contained	12
Recommendation	10
Read other in series	5
Saw review in magazine/catalogue	4
Saw review in newspaper	3
On course list	3
Saw film/play on TV	2
Mentioned on TV/radio	1

Source: Inside Book Publishing, 4th Edition

PLAYING TO THE EBOOK ADVANTAGE

Why do people buy ebooks? The decision includes multiple motivations. This 2009 chart from Bowker is still a useful guide to the varied characteristics that appeal to readers of digital books.

Source: Bowker

[A 2012 Pew survey](#) looks at the reasoning behind ebook/print book preferences.

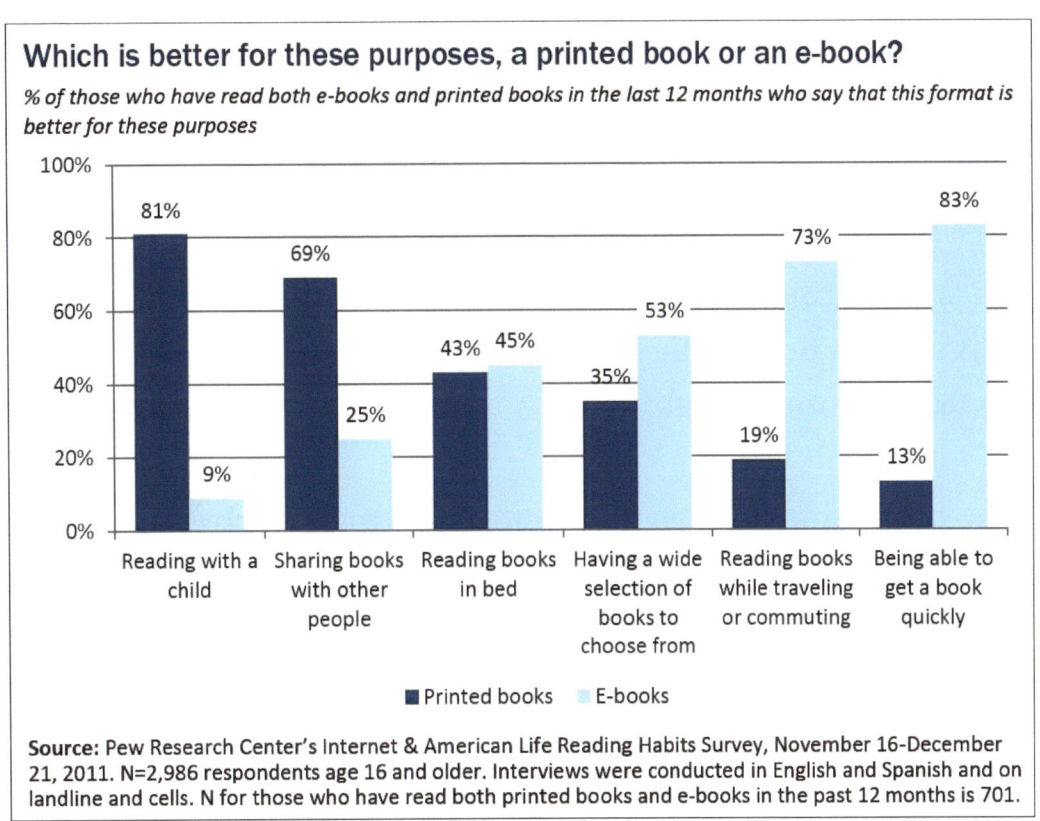

Source: Pew Research Center Internet & American Life Project

THE ONLINE ADVANTAGE

Online retailers can't match the magnificence of a book superstore when it comes to creating serendipitous awareness of important titles. But online offers unique advantages:

- An unparalleled selection of in-stock current titles, most available for 1- or 2-day delivery

- Lower prices than at most retail stores

- An extraordinary range of self-published ebooks, generally at prices lower than similar books from traditional publishers

The more profound (but tougher to measure) value of online is informing and motivating readers in ways that were rarely possible before the Internet:

- Learning more about authors and their work is just a click or two away

- Online communities bring readers and writers together

- Online retailers enable low-cost (or free) promotions, giveaways and ebook loans

- Web browsing exposes readers to more books more often

Book clubs predate the Internet but had nothing like the size and scale of online "communities of interest" today. Reaching those clubs was clumsy in those days, while today's book groups flourish specifically because of the web.

EBOOK PRICING

What's the best price for an ebook? The numerous surveys and analyses publishing in recent years offer a range of sometimes contradictory advice.

Larger publishers routinely set new ebook prices above ten dollars ($9.99) as long as the discounted hardcover price remains at least several dollars higher.

There's a separate school of thought, articulated mostly by self-published authors, that ebook prices should be closer to four dollars than to twelve dollars. Trade publishers, they say, are trying to protect their print franchises by overpricing ebooks.

Book prices have risen by as much as 7% in the last decade-and-a-half, but by 2012 they had retreated to 1998 levels (adjusted for inflation). In other words, compared to many other consumer goods, books are as affordable today as they were the year the movie *Titanic* was released. In the same period [movie prices outpaced inflation by 50%](). You could say that book prices are a bargain.

Source: U.S. Bureau of Labor Statistics

In the early days of the Kindle, Amazon subsidized the prices of newly released ebooks, maintaining them at $9.99 or lower. Sales surged. Self-published books entered the market at still lower retail prices. For the first time since the introduction of mass-market paperbacks, the industry could see the price sensitivity of book buyers. Once they dropped below a certain price, books became an impulse buy: readers who bought a book for three bucks and didn't much care if they ever read it. If they paid $11.99, the regrets could creep in.

The contractual dispute between Amazon and Hachette, which ran from May to November 2014, offered some insights into ebook pricing.

Amazon has argued repeatedly that prices as high as "$14.99 and even $19.99" are "unjustifiably high for an ebook." It says that it had "quantified the price elasticity of ebooks from repeated measurements across many titles" and that "for every copy an ebook would sell at $14.99, it would sell 1.74 copies if priced at $9.99." (Several commentators take aim at that assertion, pointing out that at least the price of the hardcover should be factored into the equation.)

Hachette defended itself, writing that "more than 80% of the ebooks we publish are priced at $9.99 or lower" and that "those few priced higher–most at $11.99 and $12.99–are less than half the price of their print versions."

MOBILE AND THE PRICING DECISION

Fingers move fast on mobile devices. If a book buyer pauses, the sale may be lost. Low-price impulse buyers have little resistance and fewer regrets.

Smashwords is the "the world's largest distributor of indie ebooks." In his 2014 Smashwords Survey CEO Mark Coker noted that ebooks priced at $.99, $2.99 and $3.99 have the highest unit sales. He writes that "the highest earning indie authors are utilizing lower average prices than the authors who earn less, but this doesn't mean that ultra-low prices such as $.99 are the path to riches. $2.99 and $3.99 are the sweet spots for most of the bestsellers." At the same time he's discovered that "non-fiction earns more at higher prices."

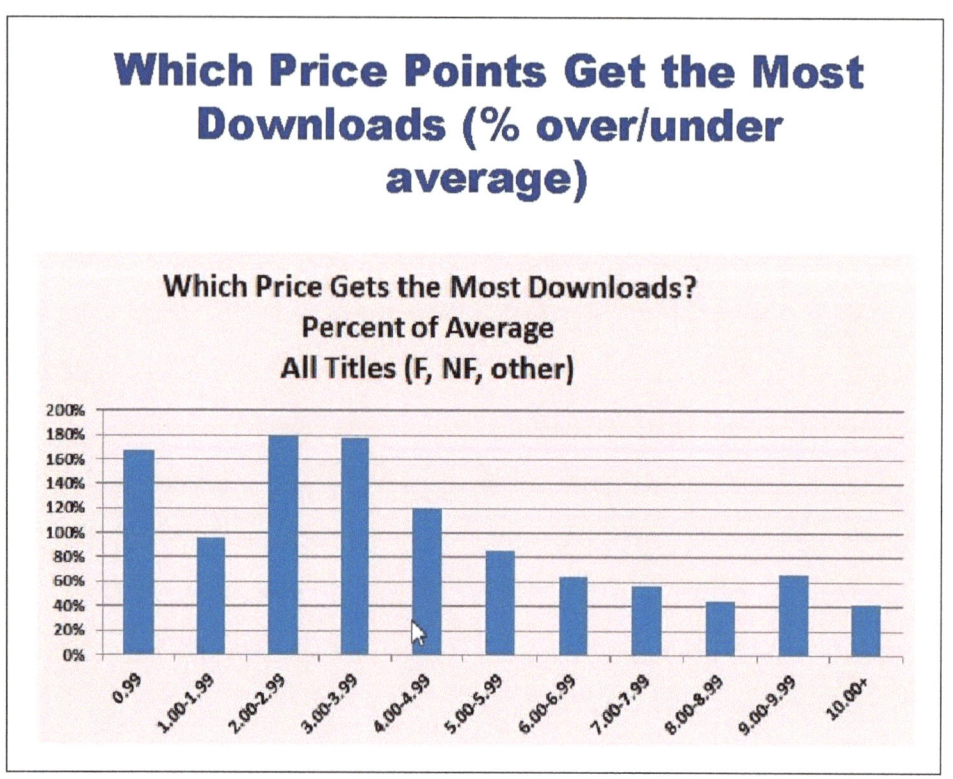

Source: 2014 Smashwords Survey

Kobo offers a detailed white paper on pricing called *Power Pricing 2014*. It shows that sales begin to tail off once the retail price moves above $9.99.

A lot of work remains to be done to find the balance of price-to-profit by book type, device, publication date, frequency of purchase and more. Perhaps there aren't three times as many users who will spend $3.99 on an ebook as would spend $11.99 for the same title. Fortunately, publishers can test new pricing strategies online, along with other variables like cover design, subject category and enhanced metadata.

THE INTERNATIONAL OPPORTUNITY

The stats in Chapter 1 of this report show that the international market for English-language ebooks is many times larger than the U.S. market (by volume, not by price). Publishers have never had direct access to so many English speakers (and to even more students of English).

Bookstats pegged total U.S. trade book sales at $15.05 billion in 2012. The Association of American Publishers (AAP) separately reported $833.4 million of book sales (all categories) "from non-U.S. markets." U.S. Commerce Department data from 2010 shows that nearly half (46.4%) of U.S. book exports go to Canada and 22% to non-English-speaking countries.

Source: The Economist

Setting an optimal ebook retail price for each country will always be a challenge. Various indices offer different guidance for assessing prices abroad. Often mentioned is The Economist's "Big Mac Index," measuring the price of a McDonald's Big Mac in countries around the world. Launched half in jest in 1986, the index has become a useful guide to understanding purchasing parity worldwide. Using the index, a publisher would determine that an ebook retailing for $9.99 in the U.S. should be priced at $7.49 in the Czech Republic, $4.99 in Indonesia, and $3.49 in India (using standard ebook price points in U.S. dollars).

Google Play now has over 50 international sites selling ebooks, as does Apple. Amazon has sites in nine countries other than the U.S. Kobo has perhaps the most international focus of all the U.S.-based resellers. While it doesn't have branded websites in nearly as many countries as Google and Apple, it claims that "each Kobo device and app supports 68 languages" and "over 12 million readers use Kobo in 190 countries."

MOBILE MARKETING'S ECOSYSTEM

Social media is synonymous with mobile, especially on smartphones. And social media now dominates consumer decision-making. In doesn't invalidate the specific reasons for book buying pictured above. Instead, social media supports those choices while offering new channels to spread the word.

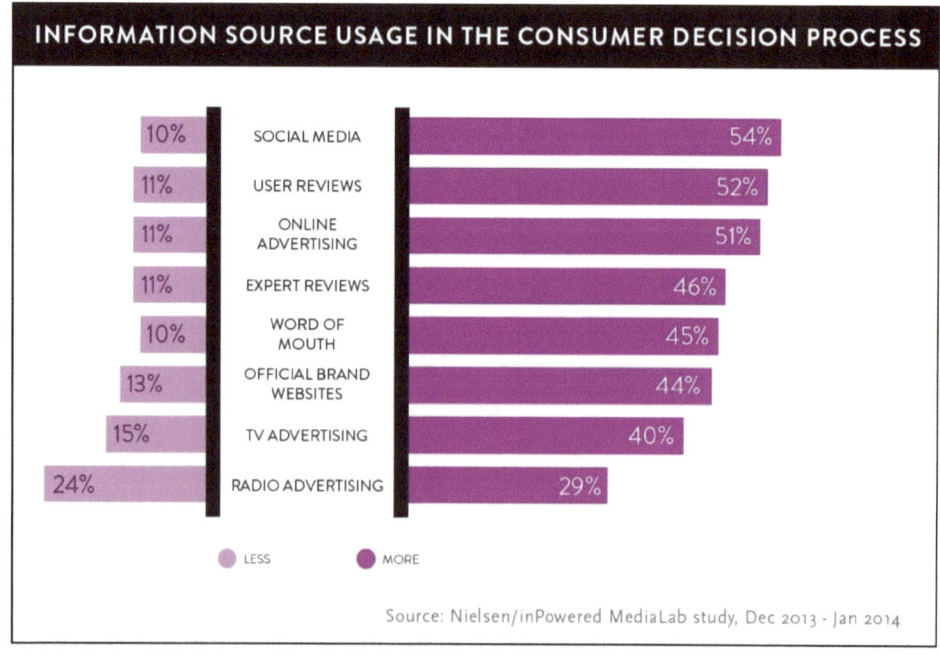

Source: Nielsen

The next charts offer guideposts for mobile marketers developing social media strategies.

The Secrets of Word-of-Mouth Marketing by George Silverman (2011) is an indispensable companion to mobile marketing. "Word-of-mouth" is a straightforward analogy for how social media influences readers and book buyers. Silverman details a spectrum of opportunities accessible in the digital universe. Each is a tool for enthusiasts to share and to draw new readers into their universe.

Social Media for Book Marketing	
Customer-generated media	Yahoo, YouTube, Pinterest
Podcasting	Search Google for best
Mobile apps	Advertising (Google AdWords), author apps
Blogs	Articles and reviews
Ratings and review sites	Goodreads, Amazon
Social networking	Facebook, Twitter, LinkedIn
Social bookmarking	Digg, StumbleUpon, Reddit
Wikis	Wikipedia, Wikibooks, Quora
Webinars	WebEx, GoToMeeting
Filesharing sites	KickassTorrents, Pirate Bay
Digital photos and video	Flickr, Instagram, Vimeo
Other e-commerce sites	eBay, Overstock

Adapted from *The Secrets of Word-of-Mouth Marketing*

On his Sideways Thoughts blog Chad Renando presents another view of the "social media taxonomy." Tools are listed in the left-hand column. The numbers ranged at the bottom of the chart estimate the popularity of each tool. For example, Twitter draws vastly more micro-bloggers than do Plurk or Yammer.

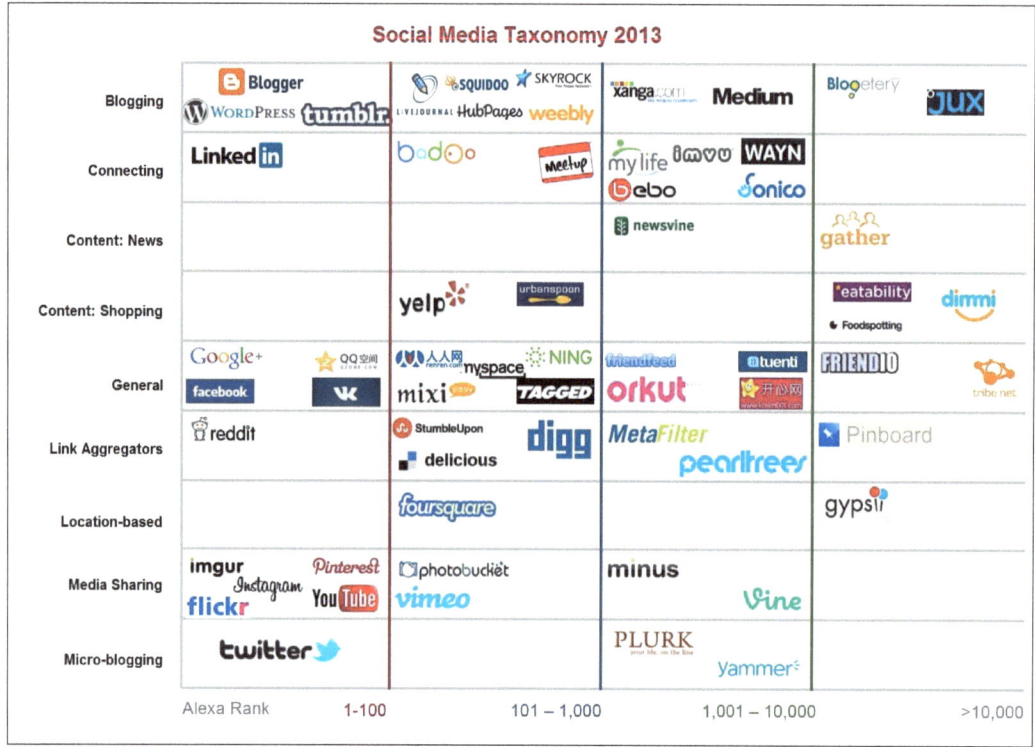

Source: Sideways Thoughts

ONLINE MEETS BRICKS-AND-MORTAR RETAIL

Mobile strategies aren't standalone efforts. They're part of a broader digital strategy, encompassing the web, email and social media. In turn, digital strategies are aligned with more traditional marketing strategies, including print reviews and advertising, author appearances and a bricks-and-mortar retail plan.

Devin Wenig, president of eBay Marketplaces, gave McKinsey a must-read interview about the future of retail in the age of mobile. "It's not about the phone or the desktop or the store—it's about all of those," he says. "They've just come together, the on- and the offline. Now, every merchant, every retailer must have an omnichannel strategy or they won't survive."

Online now accounts for nearly half of book sales (see the stats in Chapter 1). The balance comes from a combination of bookstores and mass merchandisers. Traditional book marketing techniques still apply in this world. Mobile creates another layer to engage and motivate customers.

Source: Author

Publisher and author websites can feature coupons offering discounts or bonuses. Book retailers can offer in-store coupons. Coupon Sherpa provides a handful of both book publisher and retailer coupons. Coupon Cabin has a wider assortment. Some of these online coupons highlight a couponing "no-no": touting "specials" that are already freely available at the reseller's stores or web site.

Humanitas, a publisher in Bucharest, Romania launched an imaginative program combining the physical with the digital. Posters in subway stations featured Humanitas titles. Readers selected a title from a large selection, scanned a QR code, and received a sample of the book. If they liked what they read a button linked to a site where they could buy the complete book.

Source: WebUrbanist

AUTHORS, NOT PUBLISHERS

Authors are the brand, not their publishers. This is true for most creative content. We don't buy music because it's from Sony or Universal, and we don't watch a movie because Paramount Pictures financed it. (Of course there are exceptions, like Disney.)

Successful fiction authors are tied closely to their work. Their first book is rarely a best-seller. Most authors who make it to No. 1 on the *New York Times* best-seller list have multiple titles in print. Each new title is an opportunity to build an author's brand. Writers of literary fiction tend to eschew series, but that model often works for all other fiction categories.

In nonfiction publishing, the book is more likely than the author to be the brand. In nonfiction, a first book can become a best-seller. Promoting nonfiction online relies more on the content than on the author's personality. Still, many best-selling nonfiction authors gain brand recognition when they're properly promoted.

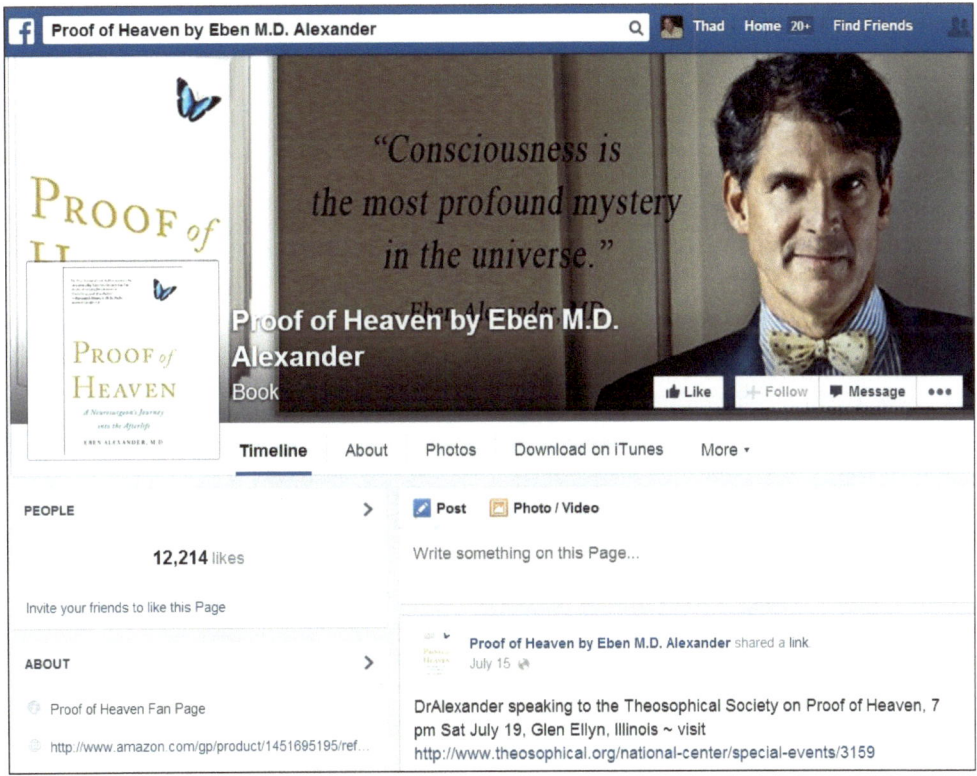

In this case the book, not the first-time author. (Source: Facebook.com)

Publishers continue to experiment with increasing consumer brand engagement (B2C). Meanwhile, William Kingsland and Rakesh Satyal make a compelling argument that publishers should invest in their brands to better serve their B2B partners, "namely, authors and the agents who represent them, as well as booksellers like Amazon and Barnes & Noble, and professional book reviewers."

APPS AND BOOK PUBLISHING

Amazon senior VP for Kindle Russ Grandinetti recently told the New York Times, "Books don't just compete against books. Books compete against Candy Crush, Twitter, Facebook, streaming movies, newspapers you can read for free. It's a new world."

Source: Amazon

Despite the million apps available for Apple and Android, too many companies still want to believe that "if we build it they will come." Novelty sold apps for the first few months after the launch of the iPhone, and again after the launch of the iPad. There's far too much clutter in app stores today to rely on discovery. App strategies are becoming increasingly detailed and sophisticated.

BROAD STROKES STRATEGIES

Seven years after the launch of the iPhone the mobile industry has enough experience to propose a few broad rules.

- The best apps offer a single core function.

- Downloading an app, free or paid, is the first step in a process. What's going to bring users back to your app again and again?

- Free is the simplest business model: 90% of apps are free. (The industry uses a term, "freemium"–free apps that try to make a sale within the app, usually for added features.)

- Apple delivers the top user experience and attracts the "high-end" market.

- With their smaller screens, smartphones apps command different designs than do tablet apps.

Additional guidelines apply particularly to publishing:

- Apps that *imitate* the book usually fail. A good app reimagines the content and exploits the features of each device.

- Content strategies differ for fiction and for nonfiction.

APPS FOR AUTHORS

Source: The author

Many app sites are chasing bands; musicians seem to have figured out how to make apps make sense. The obvious value—sharing audio & video, tweets and performance calendars—could work for authors too.

Still, there's scant evidence that apps are as yet playing an important role in author promotion and fan engagement. Mobile Roadie is one of the few app services targeting authors for its services. Sadly it highlights just a single author app in 2014 and only one so far in 2015.

CONCLUSION

Mobile marketing complements existing book marketing programs; it doesn't replace them. Marketing used to be a one-way street leading to passive listeners. Now it's an enormous network enabling conversations between and among writers and readers.

Publishers need to master new skills for mobile marketing. The best path is immersion: mobile is not for dabblers.

CHAPTER 5
CASE STUDIES: PUBLISHING GOES MOBILE

The companies and products featured in this chapter illustrate a range of mobile efforts. Three are from trade publishers, and two are from app-only publishers. Most intriguing is the mobile publishing phenomenon, Wattpad.

WATTPAD

Wattpad is the leading player in mobile book-style content creation and consumption. Its popularity offers key lessons to traditional publishers. Most telling is the domination of mobile for Wattpad users. The blurring of the line between writers and readers is just as fascinating.

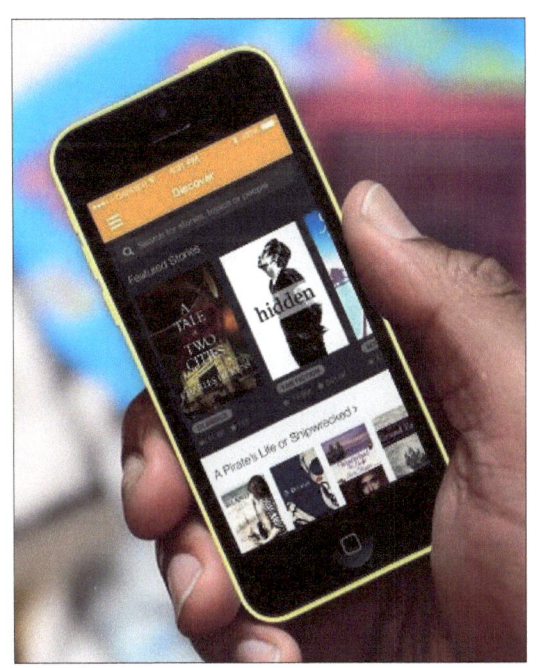

Source: Wattpad

The co-founders of Toronto-based Wattpad, Allen Lau and Ivan Yuen, did not emerge from careers in publishing. When they launched Wattpad in 2006, each had a background in mobile and wireless technology. Their initial plan was to offer classic fiction through their site: Dickens' *Tale of Two Cities* was the first upload. Customers decided what they wanted to read next. This morphed into encouraging readers to upload their own stories. Allen Lau claims that "if Charles Dickens were writing today he would be an Internet addict."

In a 2012 interview Lau said that he "believes the Kindle, and similar e-readers, are simply the bridge products, tying the digital world with 'the traditional publishing process that we got used to [in] the last 400 years." It's the same way that Microsoft's Encarta encyclopedia was a bridge between print-based volumes and Wikipedia.

Today Wattpad claims 35 million registered users and 75 million story uploads in 50 languages. *Wired* magazine's Clive Thompson, writes that "Wattpad's success may presage a shift in how fiction is written—and read—by the under-25 crowd that the site primarily serves."

Remarkably, some 85% of user access is from mobile devices, mainly smartphones. Lau notes that "for a generation that lives online, through their phones, writing is part of their entertainment. It's a hobby, and with fragmented times, when the inspiration comes you can write, right on the spot."

In January, 2014 Allen Lau delivered a lecture to Toronto's Entrepreneurship 101 program. The one-hour video is available online; the slide deck offers a condensed version of an eye-opening story of what it took this company to make it as a start-up.

TOUCH PRESS

The new truism: An app is worth a thousand words. Touch Press's apps are the proof. Here's a screenshot of its *Beethoven's 9th Symphony* app for the iPad:

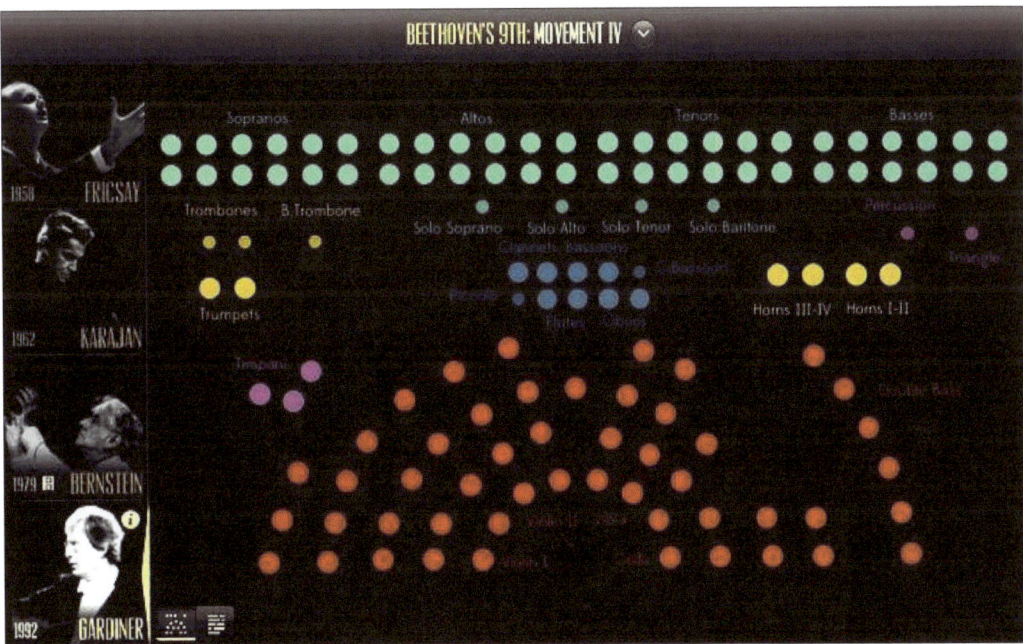

Source: Touch Press

Not much, is it? A sample of this Touch Press app can be downloaded for free. In action it's extraordinary, an exquisite combination of audio, video, music scores and animation. Revealing of Touch Press's approach was its partnership with Deutsche Grammophon. The famed classical record label is home to the four essential recordings of the *Beethoven's 9th Symphony* included in the app. Users can switch between each performance on the fly.

The app won the award for best reference digital book at the 2013 FutureBook Innovation Awards. As of June 2014, it has 968,053 downloads, remarkable for almost any "publication."

Sam Aspinall is CEO of London-based Touch Press. "We believe that the most beautiful and successful interfaces are those that showcase the content rather than stand in its way," she says. "The hardest part of what we do is making the interface invisible."

The Elements was the first app published by Touch Press. Released simultaneously with the iPad's launch in April 2010, it now has over a million downloads. The market is international: half a million dollars worth of the downloads have been in Japan. (Theodore Gray's *Molecules*, the sequel to *The Elements*, was released in November, 2014.)

There's a purity in Touch Press's approach that should inspire all bookish app developers. "Apps are often conceived as mere derivative or supporting works: 'the app version of such and such a book' or 'the app of the film'," says Aspinall. "We believe that the app can be an art form in and of itself." At the same time, the company refuses to work with preexisting app development frameworks "designed to simplify and speed up the development process."

All of Touch Press's apps use native development environments. Aspinall explains that "the reason is very simple: "We prefer to have as little as possible between the device itself and our code, so that we have more flexibility and every opportunity to squeeze out the last ounce of performance." This adds greatly to the app development cost. It's a gamble: cost versus customer delight. The gamble is paying off handsomely for Touch Press.

SIMON & SCHUSTER AUTHOR PORTAL

Announced in June 2014, the Simon & Schuster author portal, dubbed "S&S InkedIn" (not to be confused with LinkedIn, though the publisher describes the as being "accessible to authors on the popular networking site LinkedIn").

S&S InkedIn is a good example of a mobile-enabled extranet, serving partners who aren't employees of the company. LinkedIn has smartphone-optimized apps, and so S&S InkedIn is accessible to any author on any device.

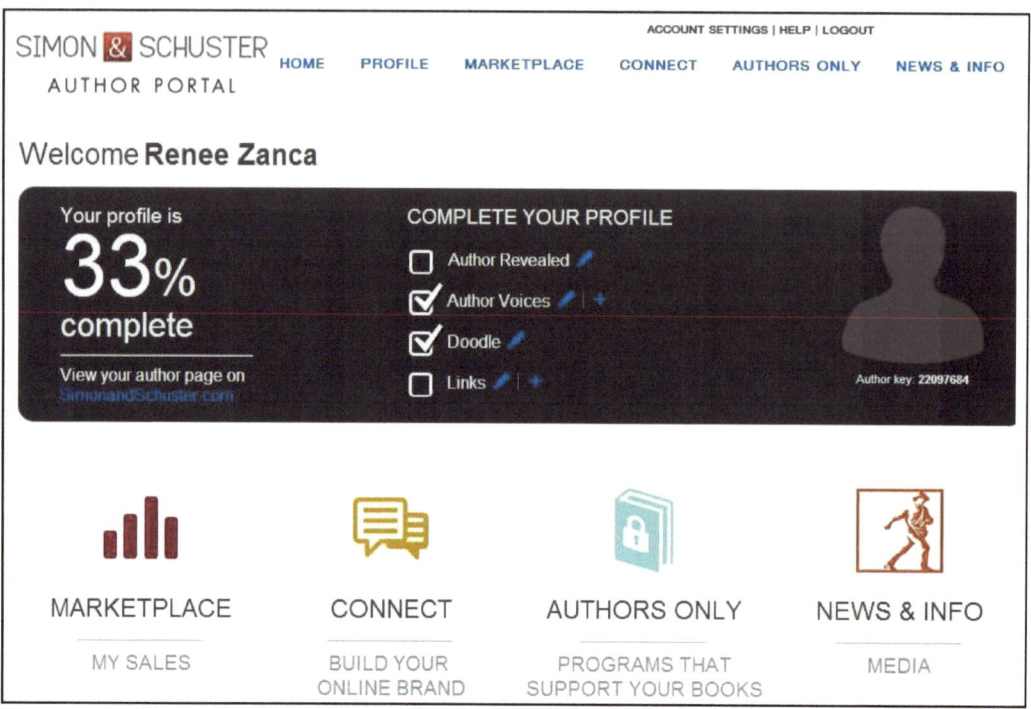

Source: Simon & Schuster

In October 2014 [Hachette announced their Author and Agent Portal](), similar to the Simon & Schuster effort. When fully deployed, it will include sales information for authors' titles, updated weekly, as well as "file sharing for easy transfer of a manuscript or other large files."

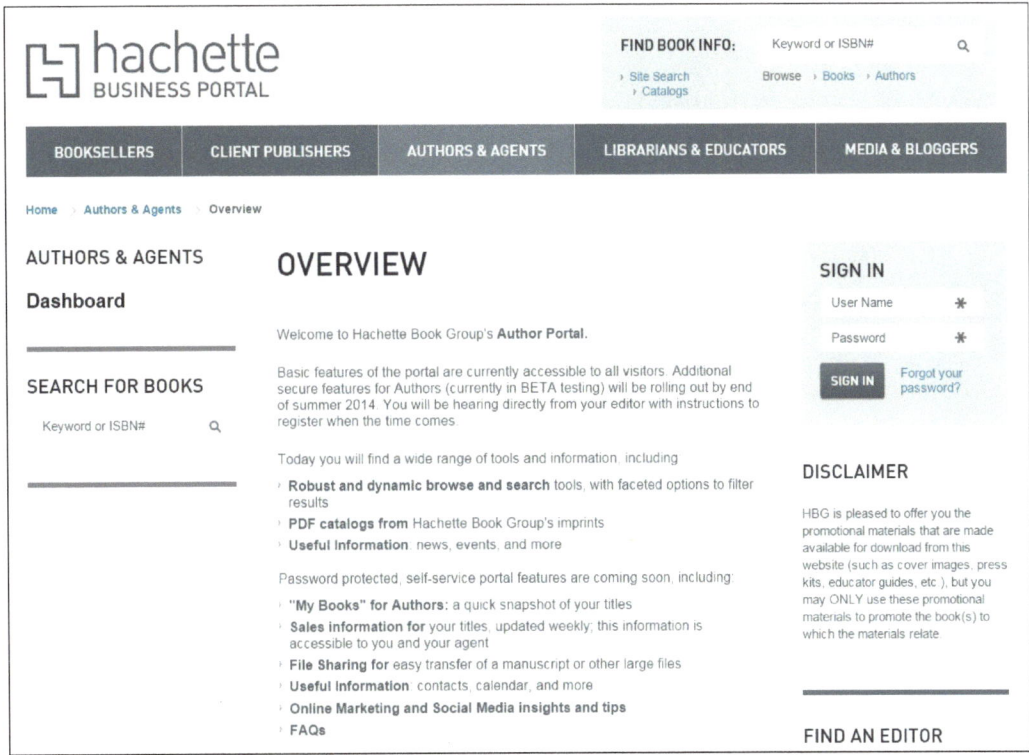

Source: Hachette

SOURCEBOOKS

When the publishing industry looks for inspiration it often turns to Sourcebooks and its dynamic founder and CEO Dominique Raccah.

Among trade book publishers Sourcebooks has been a pioneer in enhanced ebooks and apps. They offer a range of titles focused on the practical and on children. Enhanced ebook titles include:

- [An Innovative First—Country Music: The Masters](#)

- [Let Every Nation Know](#)

- [Horrid Henry](#)

- [Zone Golf](#)

- [Practical Meditation](#)

Apps include the [Fiske Interactive College Guide](#) and the very successful titles from [Put Me in the Story App](#): Best-Selling *Books Starring Your Child!*

According to Raccah, "We're having a big conversation internally right now about our app strategy. We tend to be Apple-centric/Apple-exclusive in our app program. We came out of the Apple Worldwide Developers Conference (WWDC) last June with lots of ideas for thinking about our app program differently. We've now gone through three versions of a new strategy. My guess is there's going to be much more work on this front."

HIS DREAM, OUR STORIES

His Dream, Our Stories is a fine example of how one publisher created multiple versions of a digital story, each optimized for the particular display technology.

Source: Screenshot

His Dream, Our Stories commemorates Dr. Martin Luther King, Jr. and his classic "I Have a Dream" speech on its fiftieth anniversary. Through commentary and archival footage, the digital book chronicles the March on Washington, the Civil Rights movement and the legacy of Dr. Martin Luther King, Jr. It's available for free on the Web and as a free ebook.

The enhanced ebook is available on four platforms:

- Apple iBooks
- Amazon's Kindle Fire HD
- Barnes & Noble's NOOK
- Google Play

Source: Screenshot

There's also a stripped-down version in Kindle's Mobi format that does a serviceable job of rendering the book into two dimensions.

Kirkus called the title an "excellent enhanced ebook" and "an outstanding supplement to Dr. King's speech." The Independent Book Publishers Association (IBPA) named it a Benjamin Franklin Digital Award Gold Honoree for innovation in electronic book publishing. Digital Book World awarded it a QED Seal.

The "Share Your Story" feature gives readers an opportunity to add their personal memories of the time, both in words and optionally as video in a special section of the online ebook.

TASCHEN BOOKS

The German publisher Taschen Books produces many of the world's most sumptuous art and photography books. Founded in 1980 by Benedikt Taschen (still the managing director) the company prides itself on offering beautiful books at low prices.

It publishes books on classical painters for $9.99 and collector's editions of art and photography books routinely priced at $1,000 and up. The limited and signed edition of its new Annie Leibovitz collection retails for $5,000.

The Annie Leibovitz book comes with a custom-made tripod (Source: Taschen)

With some 150 titles in print Taschen also operates thirteen branded retail stores in Europe and the U.S. At first glance this would not be a setting where ebooks thrive. Not so: the company now sells thirty ebooks and one app.

Julius Wiedemann is the director of digital publications at Taschen. He's held the role for four years; previously he was editor in charge for nine years. Wiedemann is quick to point out that creating ebooks at Taschen isn't easy. "There's a psychological reward when people buy or receive a Taschen book," he says. "This feeling is hard to recreate because e-readers won't put those books on a coffee table or a bookshelf."

On the other hand, "our books aren't easy to transport. They are not so mobile, and sometimes they're really heavy." His challenge is to "re-imagine the reward from the book's content."

He finds the most challenging task is using digital tools to reconcile the viewing experience of print. "Our big printed books offer this huge "screen," full of detail, and the object in 3D immediately conveys a notion of value," Wiedemann says. "The digital book doesn't offer that immediate depth."

William Claxton. Jazzlife includes more than 600 interactive photographs and 20 jazz songs (Source: Taschen).

Taschen hoped to publish 100 ebooks by 2014, but as yet offers only a third of that number. Quality is paramount and, says Wiedemann, "we slowed down the process to create unique products with the same demands we have for all other books, both in design and editorial." The company had been relying mostly on Apple's iBooks software. "It can take a couple of months to get one book right," Wiedemann says. "We are talking about user interface, not just page layout anymore."

At the same time it's a challenge to keep costs under control. One way is to maximize reuse of existing text and image assets. He adds audio and video where he can, aware that these "can become a distraction." He says that he won't offer multimedia for the sake of it.

Wiedemann has ambitious plans for Taschen Digital. "We plan to be everywhere," he says, "from apps to ebooks, from mobile sites to audio books."

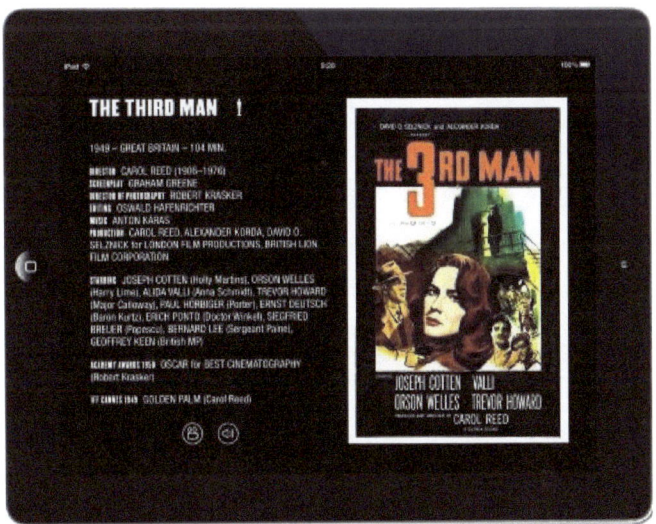

100 All-Time Favorite Movies includes trailers and soundtracks for featured films. (Source: Taschen).

CHAPTER 6
THE FUTURE OF MOBILE FOR DIGITAL PUBLISHERS

The future of mobile shines bright. Apps are becoming more sophisticated while development costs drop. New devices will enable new opportunities to feature fresh digital content.

Roughly two-thirds of Americans now own smartphones. The installed base should reach nearly 100% as smartphones continue to replace landlines. (Little-known fact: even landline phone ownership [never exceeded 96%](#)).

The outlook for tablets is hazier. Tablet madness has calmed, but there is already a huge group of users both in developed and developing markets. Phablet adoption—smartphones with screens nearly as large as on mini-tablets—represents a new product category altogether. The question, though, is whether they also represent a new market opportunity.

Android has a growing lead over Apple iOS in the worldwide market. Yet Apple mobile customers are a well-heeled bunch. They pay more for their devices, whether tablets or smartphones, and are willing to spend more money on apps, music and video content. Apple devices will remain the priority for publishers and developers for the foreseeable future.

Source: Wikimedia Commons

Windows is not much of a contender thus far and the latest IDC data shows that Windows phones are losing market share (down to 2.5% of the market). Windows tablets have not caught on either. Meanwhile, Blackberry has all but fallen off the smartphone map (0.5% market share).

Book buyers remain comfortable with digital formats that mimic print. Apps mostly fail as proxies for print books. The app opportunity for book publishers is still fuzzy. Only the children's market is app-happy. Enhanced ebooks are coming into their own and may represent the next digital content opportunity for publishers.

Books increasingly compete with other forms of entertainment, particularly because those other forms are available on the same devices used for reading. While the statistics show that people are reading as much as ever, only new forms of content will drive U.S. market growth. Growth in ebook sales will come from other countries; the international opportunity for English-language ebooks is enormous.

Most of all publishers must reimagine their role in an all-mobile, all-digital world. Emulating streaming video on demand with ebook subscription services is not remarkable. Bundling print and digital can be useful. Writing a story on Twitter is fun but not memorable. The much-anticipated breakthrough connecting writers and readers is still unknown. Will mobile technologies enable the next stage in publishing? They are certain to be front and center.

GLOSSARY

Italicized words within a definition have a separate entry.

For terms not included here please consult either http://mobileanhouraday.com/mobile-dictionary/ or the 53-page Mobile Marketing Industry Glossary ([PDF](#)), published by the [Mobile Marketing Association](#).

ANDROID

Android is Google's native operating system for smartphones and tablets. Android's underlying code is different from the code of Apple's operating system, called *iOS*. As a result developers must write separate versions of their *apps* for each system.

APP

App is an abbreviation for "application." Applications are the software, such as Microsoft Word or Adobe Photoshop, that runs on top of an *OS*. Apps refer to compact applications running on mobile devices. Apps are not as complex or powerful as applications because of the smaller screens for which they're designed. They fill just a single function such as accessing Facebook or Twitter, playing a game or taking a photograph.

CELL PHONES

See *smartphones.*

DAU

See *MAU*.

EBOOKS

Ebooks designate a digital file containing the contents of a book. Ebooks range from simple ASCII text-only version of a book, to a standard ebook format (*EPUB* or *Mobi*), to an *enhanced ebook*.

ENHANCED EBOOK

Enhanced ebooks add audio, video and/or interactive features to a book's text.

EPUB

EPUB is the industry-standard ebook format [specified by the International Digital Publishing Forum (IDPF)](). While version 3.01 is the current version, most publishers still favor the simpler [EPUB 2.0.1](). *Mobi* is Amazon's proprietary variant on EPUB 2.0.1, while Kindle Format 8 (KF8) is Amazon's proprietary response to EPUB 3.

E-READER

E-readers are portable wireless devices optimized for read books primarily comprised of text. Most e-readers use [E Ink's]() black-and-white electronic paper technology.

FEATURE PHONES

See *smartphones*.

IOS

Apple's native mobile operating system. See also *Android*.

KF8

See *EPUB*.

MAU

The most important measure of user engagement in the mobile space is the ratio of DAU:MAU, the Daily Active User(s): Monthly Active User(s). If an app is gaining traction the DAU will be larger than the MAU. Many experts rate an app as successful with a .2 ratio.

MOBI

See *EPUB*.

MOBILE

Mobile refers to the broad ecosystem of mobile devices, operating systems, apps and mobile users that are redefining the communication technology industry.

MOBILE DEVICE

A mobile device is a lightweight wireless phone, tablet or e-reader built for portability. Mobile devices let users make calls and send text messages, browse the web, read ebooks, view video and listen to audio, and to use any of over 1 million free and paid apps.

OS

OS is an abbreviation for operating system, the software that forms the underpinning for applications (on PCs) and apps (on mobile devices). The most popular mobile OSs are iOS (for Apple mobile devices) and Android (Google's mobile OS), used on most other mobile devices.

PC

Personal Computers (PCs) appear in three forms: desktop PCs (stationary devices), portable PCs (carry them with you) and notebook PCs (small portable PCs). (Tablets are often called tablet PCs; in this instance the term *tablet* is more important than the term PC.) While mobile is now the faster-growing market, there are already [over 1.5 billion PCs in use worldwide](#).

PHABLETS

A phablet is a handset with a screen size between 5 and 7 inches. Phablets are crossover devices functioning both as phones and tablets.

SMARTPHONES

All smartphones are cell phones, in that they connect to the phone network not with wires but through a series of radio transmitters. While cell phones might have just a text interface, smartphones use high-resolution touch screens and offer a wide range of apps through an online store. Cell phones are often called feature phones.

TABLET OR TABLET PC

A tablet PC is a mobile computer with a high-resolution touch screen as the input device. Screen sizes usually range between 7 and 10 inches. While they can function for general computing tasks (often with optional keyboards), tablets are most often used for media consumption, in particular video and games.

WEB APP

Web apps run in web browsers rather than as small standalone software programs. As such they're best suited to PCs and tablets; smartphones aren't optimal for web display. [Bubblewrap](#) is a simple game app that runs on Google's Chrome browser.

ADDITIONAL RESOURCES

BOOKS AND REPORTS

- Mobile Marketing: *How Mobile Technology Is Revolutionizing Marketing, Communications and Advertising*
By Daniel Rowles. Published November, 2013.
A solid overview of the important topics in mobile marketing. Free sample of the TOC, intro and Chapter 2 can be downloaded, as can Chapter 11. The author's website offers additional resources: http://www.targetinternet.com/

- Mobile Marketing: An Hour a Day
Splitting the topic into bite-sized chunks makes it more digestible. By Noah Elkin and Rachel Pasqua. Published December 2012. The TOC as well as Chapters 1 and 10 are free on SlideShare. Author website, with additional resources: http://mobileanhouraday.com/

- The New Rules of Marketing & PR: *How to Use Social Media, Online Video, Mobile Applications, Blogs, News Releases, and Viral Marketing to Reach Buyers Directly, 4th Ed.*
By David Meerman Scott. Published July 2013. The book is particularly useful because it places mobile within the broader digital marketing context.
Author website: http://www.davidmeermanscott.com/books/the-new-rules-of-marketing-and-pr/

WEBSITES

- Marketing Land (102,000 Twitter followers) is the best website covering mobile marketing (as part of much broader coverage of digital marketing). Its sister site, Search Engine Land (283,000 Twitter followers) is widely accepted as the leading information source on the topic.

- Mobile Web, from Wikipedia. Thorough.

- Mobile Marketing Association (MMA)
  "The MMA's mission is to accelerate the transformation and innovation of marketing through mobile, driving business growth with closer and stronger consumer engagement."

- The London School of Marketing features online courses in digital marketing.

- Webbiquity provides a comprehensive online directory of the top marketing and advertising news sources categorized by country and subject.

EXPERTS

There is no shortage of bright lights sharing marketing insights for a digital world. Seth Godin, Brian Solis, Mitch Joel and more are well worth following.

The book publishing industry now has its own bright light. Pete McCarthy, with a deep background in publishing marketing, has emerged as the expert on digital strategies. His services don't come cheap—$3,000-$5,000 per session. Fortunately some of his insights are accessible online. The slides from his seminar, *Big Ideas from Big (or Small) Data*, open a window into the world of advanced analytics. In a brief report, Book Marketing & Social Media FAQ, McCarthy addresses core questions on digital marketing strategies.

ABOUT THE AUTHOR

Thad McIlroy is an electronic publishing analyst and author based in San Francisco and Vancouver.

Source: The Author

His site, www.thefutureofpublishing.com, is the most thorough exploration of where publishing is headed. McIlroy provides consulting services to publishing and media companies, design and advertising agencies, as well as the full range of vendors serving the publishing industry. Having authored a dozen books and over 300 articles on these subjects, he serves also as an expert witness on patent litigation in the media industries. McIlroy served also for five years as Program Director for Seybold Seminars.

McIlroy is on the editorial board of the journal Learned Publishing and the Canadian literary journal, Geist. He is a member of the Association for Computing Machinery (ACM) and the Technical Association of the Graphic Arts (TAGA). His latest book (co-authored) is The Metadata Handbook: A Book Publisher's Guide to Creating and Distributing Metadata for Print and Ebooks.

Thad McIlroy's listing on LinkedIn.

ABOUT THE SPONSOR

Integra is one of the leading digital content services companies providing content enrichment and learning transformation services to publishers and educational institutions while also providing workplace learning and development solutions for enterprises.

Headquartered in Pondicherry, India, Integra has its global service delivery centers in India, Japan and the US besides providing project management & editorial support out of UK, Spain and Italy. Integra is the principal sponsor of this report. For more information, visit www.integra.co.in.

www.ingramcontent.com/pod-product-compliance
Lightning Source LLC
Chambersburg PA
CBHW041544220426
43665CB00002B/32